Famous Imposters

Bram Stoker

FAMOUS IMPOSTORS

BY

BRAM STOKER

AUTHOR OF "DRACULA," "PERSONAL REMINISCENCES OF HENRY IRVING," ETC., ETC.

ILLUSTRATED

New York

STURGIS & WALTON COMPANY

1910

Set up and electrotyped. Published November, 1910

PREFACE

The subject of imposture is always an interesting one, and impostors in one shape or another are likely to flourish as long as human nature remains what it is, and society shows itself ready to be gulled. The historics of famous cases of imposture in this book have been grouped together to show that the art has been practised in many forms —impersonators, pretenders, swindlers, and humbugs of all kinds; those who have masqueraded in order to acquire wealth, position, or fame, and those who have done so merely for the love of the art. So numerous are instances, indeed, that the book cannot profess to exhaust a theme which might easily fill a dozen volumes; its purpose is simply to collect and record a number of the best known instances. The author, nevertheless, whose largest experience has lain in the field of fiction, has aimed at dealing with his material as with the material for a novel, except that all the facts given are real and authentic. He has made no attempt to treat the subject ethically; yet from a study of these impostors, the objects they had in view, the means they adopted, the risks they ran, and the punishments which attended exposure, any reader can draw his own conclusions.

Impostors of royalty are placed first on account of the fascinating glamour of the throne which has allured so many to the attempt. Perkin Warbeck began a life of royal imposture at the age of seventeen and yet got an army round him and dared to make war on Harry Hotspur before ending his short and stormy life on the gallows. With a crown for stake, it is not surprising that men have been found willing to run even such risks as those taken by the impostors of Sebastian of Portugal and Louis XVII of France. That imposture, even if unsuccessful, may be very difficult to detect, is shown in the cases of Princess Olive and Cagliostro, and in those of Hannah Snell, Mary East, and the many women who in military and naval, as well as in civil, life assumed and maintained even in the din of battle the simulation of men.

One of the most extraordinary and notorious impostures ever known was that of Arthur Orton, the Tichborne Claimant, whose ultimate exposure necessitated the employment, at great public expense of time and money, of the best judicial and forensic wits in a legal process of unprecedented length.

The belief in witches, though not extinct in our country even to-day, affords examples of the converse of imposture, for in the majority of cases it was the superstitions of society which attributed powers of evil to innocent persons whose subsequent mock-trials and butchery made a public holiday for their so-called judges.

The long-continued doubt as to the true sex of the Chevalier D'Eon shows how a belief, no matter how groundless, may persist. Many cases of recent years may also be called in witness as to the initial credulity of the public, and to show how obstinacy maintains a belief so begun. The Humbert case—too fresh in the public memory to demand treatment here—the Lemoine case, and the long roll of other fraudulent efforts to turn the credulity of others to private gain, show how widespread is the criminal net, and how daring and persevering are its manipulators.

The portion of the book which deals with the tradition of the "Bisley Boy" has had, as it demanded, more full and detailed treatment than any other one subject in the volume. Needless to say, the author was at first glance inclined to put the whole story aside as almost unworthy of serious attention, or as one of those fanciful matters which imagination has elaborated out of the records of the past. The work which he had undertaken had, however, to be done, and almost from the very start of earnest enquiry it became manifest that here was a subject which could not be altogether put aside or made light of. There were too many circumstances—matters of exact record, striking in themselves and full of some strange mystery, all pointing to a conclusion which one almost feared to grasp as a possibility—to allow the question to be relegated to the region of accepted myth. A little preliminary work amongst books and maps seemed to indicate that so far from the matter, vague and inchoate as it was, being chimerical, it was one for the most patient examination. It looked, indeed, as if those concerned in making public the local tradition, which had been buried or kept in hiding somewhere for three centuries, were on the verge of a discovery of more than national importance. Accordingly, the author, with the aid of some friends at Bisley and its neighbourhood, went over the ground, and, using his eyes and ears, came to his own conclusions. Further study being thus necessitated, the subject seemed to open out in a natural way. One after another the initial difficulties appeared to find their own solutions and to vanish; a more searching investigation of the time and circumstances showed that there was little if any difficulty in the way of the story being true in essence if not in detail. Then, as point after point arising from others already examined, assisted the story, probability began to take the place of possibility; until the whole gradually took shape as a chain, link resting in the strength of link and forming a cohesive whole. That this story impugns the identity—and more than the identity—of Queen Elizabeth, one of the most famous and glorious rulers whom the world has seen, and hints at an explanation of circumstances in the life of that monarch which have long puzzled historians, will entitle it to the most serious consideration. In short, if it be true, its investigation will tend to disclose the greatest imposture known to history; and to this end no honest means should be neglected.

B. S.

CONTENTS

CONTENTS

ILLUSTRATIONS

FAMOUS IMPOSTORS

A. PERKIN WARBECK

RICHARD III literally carved his way to the throne of England. It would hardly be an exaggeration to say that he waded to it through blood. Amongst those who suffered for his unscrupulous ambition were George Duke of Clarence, his own elder brother, Edward Prince of Wales, who on the death of Edward IV was the natural successor to the English throne, and the brother of the latter, Richard Duke of York. The two last mentioned were the princes murdered in the Tower by their malignant uncle. These three murders placed Richard Duke of Gloucester on the throne, but at a cost of blood as well as of lesser considerations which it is hard to estimate. Richard III left behind him a legacy of evil consequences which was far-reaching. Henry VII, who succeeded him, had naturally no easy task in steering through the many family complications resulting from the long-continued "Wars of the Roses"; but Richard's villany had created a new series of complications on a more ignoble, if less criminal, base. When Ambition, which deals in murder on a wholesale scale, is striving its best to reap the results aimed at, it is at least annoying to have the road to success littered with the débris of lesser and seemingly unnecessary crimes. Fraud is socially a lesser evil than murder; and after all—humanly speaking—much more easily got rid of. Thrones and even dynasties were in the melting pot between the reigns of Edward III and Henry VII; so there were quite sufficient doubts and perplexities to satisfy the energies of any aspirant to royal honours—however militant he might be. Henry VII's time was so far unpropitious that he was the natural butt of all the shafts of unscrupulous adventure. The first of these came in the person of Lambert Simnel, the son of a baker, who in 1486 set himself up as Edward Plantagenet, Earl of Warwick—then a prisoner in the Tower—son of the murdered Duke of Clarence. It was manifestly a Yorkist plot, as he was supported by Margaret Duchess Dowager of Burgundy (sister of Edward IV) and others. With the assistance of the Lord-Deputy (the Earl of Kildare) he was crowned in Dublin as King Edward VI. The pretensions of Simnel were overthrown by the exhibition of the real Duke of Warwick, taken from prison for the purpose. The attempt would have been almost comic but that the effects were tragic. Simnel's span of notoriety was only a year, the close of which was attended with heavy slaughter

PERKIN WARBECK

of his friends and mercenaries. He himself faded into the obscurity of the minor life of the King's household to which he was contemptuously relegated. In fact the whole significance of the plot was that it was the first of a series of frauds consequent on the changes of political parties, and served as a *balon d'essai* for the more serious imposture of Perkin Warbeck some five years afterwards. It must, however, be borne in mind that Simnel was a pretender on his own account and not in any way a "pacemaker" for the later criminal; he was in the nature of an unconscious forerunner, but without any ostensible connection. Simnel went his way, leaving, in the words of the kingly murderer his uncle, the world free for his successor in fraud "to bustle in."

The battle of Stoke, near Newark—the battle which saw the end of the hopes of Simnel and his upholders—was fought on 16 June, 1487. Five years afterwards Perkin Warbeck made his appearance in Cork as Richard Plantagenet Duke of York. The following facts regarding him and his life previous to 1492 may help to place the reader in a position to understand other events and to find causes through the natural gateway of effects.

To Jehan Werbecque (or Osbeck as he was called in Perkin's "confession"), Controller of the town of Tournay in Picardy, and his wife, *née* Katherine de Faro, was born in 1474, a son christened Pierrequin and later known as Perkin Warbeck. The Low Countries in the fifteenth century were essentially manufacturing and commercial, and, as all countries were at that period of necessity military, growing youths were thus in touch at many points with commerce, industry and war. Jehan Werbecque's family was of the better middle class, as witness his own position and employment; and so his son spent the earlier years of his life amid scenes and conditions conducive to ambitious dreams. He had an uncle John Stalyn of Ghent. A maternal aunt was married to Peter Flamme, Receiver of Tournay and also Dean of the Guild of Schelde Boatmen. A cousin, John Steinbeck, was an official of Antwerp.

In the fifteenth century Flanders was an important region in the manufacturing and commercial worlds. It was the centre of the cloth industry; and the coming and going of the material for the clothing of the world made prosperous the shipmen not only of its own waters but those of others. The ships of the pre-Tudor navy were small affairs and of light draught suitable for river traffic, and be sure that the Schelde with its facility of access to the then British port of Calais, to Lille, to Brussels, to Bruges, to Tournai, Ghent, and Antwerp, was often itself a highway to the scenes of Continental and British wars.

About 1483 or 1484, on account of the Flemish War, Pierrequin left Tournay, proceeding to Antwerp, and to Middleburg, where he took service with a merchant, John Strewe, he being then a young boy of ten or twelve. His next move was to Portugal, whither he went with the wife of Sir Edward Brampton, an adherent of the House of York. A good deal of his early life is told in his own confession made whilst he was a prisoner in the Tower about 1497.

In Portugal he was for a year in the service of a Knight named Peter Vacz de Cogna, who, according to a statement in his confession, had only one eye. In the Confession he also states in a general way that with de Cogna he visited other countries. After this he was with a Breton merchant, Pregent Meno, of whom he states incidentally: "he made me learn English." Pierrequin Werbecque must have been a precocious boy—if all his statements are true—for when he went to Ireland in 1491 with Pregent Meno he was only seventeen years of age, and there had been already crowded into his life a fair amount of the equipment for enterprise in the shape of experience, travel, languages, and so forth.

It is likely that, to some extent at all events, the imposture of Werbecque, or Warbeck, was forced on him in the first instance, and was not a free act on his own part. His suitability to the part he was about to play was not altogether his own doing. Nay, it is more than possible that his very blood aided in the deception. Edward IV is described as a handsome debonair young man, and Perkin

Warbeck it is alleged, bore a marked likeness to him. Horace Walpole indeed in his *Historic Doubts* builds a good deal on this in his acceptance of his kingship. Edward was notoriously a man of evil life in the way of affairs of passion, and at all times the way of ill-doing has been made easy for a king. Any student of the period and of the race of Plantagenet may easily accept it as fact that the trend of likelihood if not of evidence is that Perkin Warbeck was a natural son of Edward IV. Three hundred years later the infamous British Royal Marriage Act made such difficulties or inconveniences as beset a king in the position of Edward IV unnecessary: but in the fifteenth century the usual way out of such messes was ultimately by the sword. Horace Walpole, who was a clever and learned man, was satisfied that the person who was known as Perkin Warbeck was in reality that Richard Duke of York who was supposed to have been murdered in the Tower in 1483 by Sir James Tyrrell, in furtherance of the ambitious schemes of his uncle. At any rate the people in Cork in 1491 insisted on receiving Perkin as of the House of York—at first as a son of the murdered Duke of Clarence. Warbeck took oath to the contrary before the Mayor of Cork; whereupon the populace averred that he was a natural son of Richard III. This, too, having been denied by the newcomer, it was stated that he was the son of the murdered Duke of York.

It cannot be denied that the Irish people were in this matter as unstable as they were swift in their judgments, so that their actions are really not of much account. Five years before they had received the adventurer Lambert Simnel as their king, and he had been crowned at Dublin. In any case the allegations of Warbeck's supporters did not march with established facts of gynecology. The murdered Duke of York was born in 1472, and, as not twenty years elapsed between this period and Warbeck's appearance in Ireland, there was not time in the ordinary process of nature, for father and son to have arrived at such a quality of manhood that the latter was able to appear as full grown. Even allowing for an unusual swiftness of growth common sense evidently rebelled at this, and in 1492 Perkin Warbeck was received in his final semblance of the Duke of York, himself younger son of Edward IV. Many things were possible at a period when the difficulties of voyage and travel made even small distances insuperable. At the end of the fifteenth century Ireland was still so far removed from England that even Warbeck's Irish successes, emphasised though they were by the Earls of Desmond and Kildare and a numerous body of supporters, were unknown in England till considerably later. This is not strange if one will consider that not until centuries later was there a regular postal system, and that nearly two centuries later the Lord Chief Justice Sir Matthew

Hale, who was a firm believer in witchcraft, would have condemned such a thing as telegraphy as an invention of the Devil.

In the course of a historical narrative like the present it must be borne in mind (amongst other things) that in the fifteenth century, men ripened more quickly than in the less strenuous and more luxurious atmosphere of our own day. Especially in the Tudor epoch physical gifts counted for far more than is now possible; and as early (and too often sudden) death was the general lot of those in high places, the span of working life was prolonged rather by beginning early than by finishing late. Even up to the time of the Napoleonic Wars, promotion was often won with a rapidity that would seem like an ambitious dream to young soldiers of to-day. Perkin Warbeck, born in 1474, was nineteen years of age in 1493, at which time the Earl of Kildare spoke of "this French lad," yet even then he was fighting King Henry VII, the Harry Richmond who had overthrown at Bosworth the great and unscrupulous Richard III. It must also be remembered for a proper understanding of his venture, that Perkin Warbeck was strongly supported and advised with great knowledge and subtlety by some very resolute and influential persons. Amongst these, in addition to his Irish "Cousins" Kildare and Desmond, was Margaret, Duchess of Burgundy, sister of Edward IV, who helped the young adventurer in his plot by "coaching" him up in the part which he was to play, to such an extent that, according to Lord Bacon, he was familiar with the features of his alleged family and relatives and even with the sort of questions likely to be asked in this connection. In fact he was, in theatrical parlance, not only properly equipped but "letter-perfect" in his part. Contemporary authority gives as an additional cause for this personal knowledge, that the original Jehan de Warbecque was a converted Jew, brought up in England, of whom Edward IV was the godfather. In any case it may in this age be accepted as a fact that there was between Edward IV and Perkin Warbeck so strong a likeness as to suggest a *prima facie* possibility, if not a probability, of paternity. Other possibilities crowd in to the support of such a guess till it is likely to achieve the dimensions of a belief. Even without any accuracy of historical detail there is quite sufficient presumption to justify guess-work on general lines. It were a comparatively easy task to follow the lead of Walpole and create a new "historic doubt" after his pattern, the argument of which would run thus:

After the battles of Barnet and Tewkesbury in 1471, Edward IV had but little to contend against. His powerful foes were all either dead or so utterly beaten as to be powerless for effective war. The Lancastrian hopes had disappeared with the death of Henry VI in the Tower. Margaret of Anjou (wife of Henry VI) defeated at Tewkesbury, was in prison. Warwick had been slain at Barnet, and so far as fighting was concerned, King Edward had a prolonged holiday. It was these years of peace—when the coming and going of even a king was unrecorded with that precision which marks historical accuracy—that made the period antecedent to Perkin's birth. Perkin bore an unmistakable likeness to Edward IV. Not merely that resemblance which marks a family or a race but an individual likeness. Moreover the young manhood of the two ran on parallel lines. Edward was born in 1442, and in 1461, before he was nineteen, won the battle of Mortimer's Cross which, with Towton, placed him on the throne. Perkin Warbeck at seventeen made his bid for royalty. It is hardly necessary to consider what is a manifest error in Perkin's Confession—that he was only nine years old, not eleven, at the time of the murder of Edward V. Nineteen was young enough in all conscience to begin an intrigue for a crown; but if the Confession is to be accepted as gospel this would make him only seventeen at the time of his going to Ireland—a manifest impossibility. Any statement regarding one's own birth is manifestly not to be relied on. At best such can only be an assertion *minus* the possibility of testing whence an error might come. Regarding his parentage, in case it may be alleged that there is no record of the wife of Jehan Warbecque having been in England, it may be allowed to re-

EDWARD IV AS A YOUNG MAN

call a story which Alfred, Lord Tennyson used to say was amongst the hundred best stories. It ran thus:

> A noble at the Court of Louis XIV was extremely like the King, who on its being pointed out to him sent for his double and asked him:
>
> "Was your mother ever at Court?"
>
> Bowing low, he replied:
>
> "No, sire; but my father was!"

Of course Perkin Warbeck's real adventures, in the sense of dangers, began after his claim to be the brother of Edward V was put forward. Henry VII was not slow in taking whatever steps might be necessary to protect his crown; there had been but short shrift for Lambert Simnel, and Perkin Warbeck was a much more dangerous aspirant. When Charles VIII invited him to Paris, after the war with France had broken out, Henry besieged Boulogne and made a treaty under which Perkin Warbeck was dismissed from France. After making an attempt to capture Waterford, the adventurer transferred the scene of his endeavours from Ireland to Scotland which offered him greater possibilities for intrigue on account of the struggles between James IV and Henry VII. James, who finally found it necessary to hasten his departure, seemed to believe really in his pretensions, for he gave him in marriage a kinswoman of his own, Catherine Gordon, daughter of the Earl of Huntly—who by the way was re-married no less than three times after Perkin Warbeck's death. Through the influence of Henry VII, direct or indirect, Perkin had to leave Scotland as he had been previously forced from Burgundy and the Low Countries. Country after country having been closed to him, he made desperate efforts in Cornwall, where he captured St. Michael's Mount, and in Devon, where he laid siege to Exeter. This however being raised by the Royal forces, he sought sanctuary in Beaulieu in the New Forest where, on promise of his life, he surrendered. He was sent to the Tower and well treated; but on attempting to escape thence a year later, 1499, he was taken. He was hanged at Tyburn in the same year.

Pierrequin Warbecque's enterprise was in any case a desperate one and bound to end tragically—unless, of course, he could succeed in establishing his (alleged) claim to the throne in law and then in supporting it at great odds. The latter would necessitate his vanquishing two desperate fighting men both of them devoid of fear or scruples. —Richard III and Henry VII. In any case he had the Houses of Lancaster, Plantagenet and Tudor against him and he fought with the rope round his neck.

An Act of Parliament, 1 Richard III, Cap. 15, made at Westminster on the 23 Jan., 1485, precluded all possibility—even if Warbeck should have satisfied the nation of his identity—of a legal claim to the throne, for it forbade any recognition of the offspring of Lady Elizabeth Grey to whom Edward IV was secretly married, in May, 1464, the issue of which marriage were Edward V and his brother, Richard. The act is short and is worth reading, if only for its quaint phraseology.

Cap XV. Item for certayn great causes and consideracions touchynge the suretye of the kynges noble persone as of this realme, by the advyce and assente of his lordes spirituall and temporal, and the commons in this present parliament assembled, and by the auctorite of the same. It is ordeined established and enacted, that all letters patentes, states confrymacions and actes of parlyament of anye castels seignowries, maners, landes, tenementes, fermes, fee fermes, franchises, liberties, or other hereditamentes made at any tyme to Elizabeth late wyfe of syr John Gray Knight; and now late callinge her selfe queene of England, by what so ever name or names she be called in the same, shalbe from the fyrst day of May last past utterly voyd, adnulled and of no strengthe nor effecte in the lawe. And that no person or persons bee charged to our sayde soveraygne lord the Kynge, nor to the sayde Elyzabeth, of or for any issues, prifites, or revenues of any of the sayde seignowries, castelles, maners, landes, tenementes, fermes or other hereditamentes nor for any trespas or other intromittynge in the same, nor for anye by suretye by persone or persones to her or to her use—made by them before the sayde fyrst daie of May last passed, but shalbe therof agaynste the sayd Kynge and the sayde Elizabeth clerly discharged and acquyte forever."[1]

[1] In the above memorandum no statement is made regarding Jane Shore, though it may be that she had much to do with Perkin Warbeck.

,B. THE HIDDEN KING

THE personality, nature and life of Sebastian, King of Portugal, lent themselves to the strange structure of events which followed his strenuous and somewhat eccentric and stormy life. He was born in 1554, and was the son of Prince John and his wife Juana, daughter of the Emperor Charles V. He succeeded his grandfather, John III, at the age of three. His long minority aided the special development of his character. The preceptor appointed to rule his youth was a Jesuit, Luiz-Goncalvoz de Camara. Not unnaturally his teacher used his position to further the religious aims and intrigues of his strenuous Order. Sebastian was the kind of youth who is beloved by his female relatives—quite apart from his being a King; and naturally he was treated by the women in a manner to further his waywardness. When he was fourteen years old he was crowned. From thence on he insisted on having his way in everything, and grew into a young manhood which was of the type beloved of an adventurous people. He was thus described:

"He was a headstrong violent nature, of reckless courage, of boundless ambition founded on a deep religious feeling. At the time of his coronation he was called 'Another Alexander.' He loved all kinds of danger, and found a keen pleasure in going out in a tempest in a small boat and in actually running under the guns of his own forts where his commands were stringent that any vessel coming in shore should be fired on. He was a notable horseman and could steer his charger efficiently by the pressure of either knee—indeed he was of such muscular vigour that he could, by the mere stringency of the pressure of his knees, make a powerful horse tremble and sweat. He was a great swordsman, and quite fearless. 'What is fear?' he used to say. Restless by nature he hardly knew what it was to be tired."

And yet this young man—warrior as he was, had a feminine cast of face; his features were symmetrically formed with just sufficient droop in the lower lip to give the characteristic 'note' of Austrian physiognomy. His complexion was as fine and transparent as a girl's; his eyes were clear and of blue; his hair of reddish gold. His height was medium, his figure fine; he was vigorous and active. He had an air of profound gravity and stern enthusiasm. Altogether he was, even without his Royal state, just such a young man as might stand for the idol of a young maid's dream.

And yet he did not seem much of a lover. When, in 1576, he entered Spain to meet Philip II at Guadaloupe to ask the hand of the Infanta Isabella in marriage, he was described as "cold as a wooer as he was ardent as a warrior." His eyes were so set on ambition that mere woman's beauty did not seem to attract him. Events—even that event, the meeting—fostered his ambition. When he knelt to his host, the elder king kissed him and addressed him as "Your Majesty" the first time the great title had been used to a Portuguese king. The effect must have come but little later for at that meeting he kissed the hand of the old warrior, the Duke of Alva, and uncovered to him. His underlying pride, however, was shewn at the close of that very meeting, for he claimed equal rights in formality with the Spanish king; and there was a danger that the visit of ceremony might end worse than it began. Neither king would enter the carriage in which they were to proceed together, until the host suggested that as there were two doors they should enter at the same time.

Sebastian's religious fervour and military ambition became one when he conceived the idea of renewing the Crusades; he would recover the Holy Land from the dominion of the Paynim and become himself master of Morocco in the doing of it. With the latter object in his immediate view, he made in 1574, against the wise counsels of Queen Catherine, a *sortie de reconnaissance* of the African coast; but without any result—except the fixing of his resolution to proceed. In 1578 his scheme was complete. He would listen to no warning or counsel on the subject even from the Pope, the Grand Duke of Tuscany, or the Duke of Nassau. He seemed to foresee the realization of his dreams, and would forego nothing. He gathered an army of some 18,000 men (of which less than 2,000 were horsemen) and about a dozen cannon. The preparation was made with great splendour—a sort of forerunner of the Great Armada. It seemed to be, as in the case of the projected invasion of England ten years later by Spain, a case of "counting the chickens before they were hatched."

Some indication of the number of adventurers and camp followers accompanying the army is given by the fact that the 800 craft ordained for the invasion of Morocco carried in all some 24,000 persons, inclusive of the fighting men. The paraphernalia and officials of victory comprised amongst many other luxuries: lists for jousts, a crown ready for the new King of Morocco to put on, and poets with completed poems celebrating victory.

At this time Morocco was entering on the throes of civil war. Muley Abd-el-Mulek, the reigning Sultan, was opposed by his nephew, Mohammed, and to aid the latter, who promised to bring in 400 horsemen, was the immediate object of Sebastian. But the fiery young King of Portugal had undertaken more than he was able to perform. Abd-el-Mulek opposed his 18,000 Portuguese with 55,000 Moors, (of whom 36,000 were horsemen) and with three times his number of cannon. The young Crusader's generalship was distinctly defective; he was a fine fighting man, but a poor commander. Instead of attacking at once on his arrival and so putting the zeal of his own troops and the discouragement of the enemy to the best advantage, he wasted nearly a week in hunting parties and ineffectual manœuvring. When finally issue was joined, Abd-el-Mulek, though he was actually dying, surrounded the Portuguese forces and cut them to pieces. Sebastian, though he fought like a lion, and had three horses killed under him, was hopelessly beaten. There was an attendant piece of the grimmest comedy on record. The Sultan died during the battle, but he was a stern old warrior, and as he fell back in his litter he put his finger on his lip to order with his last movement that his death should be kept secret for the time being. The officer beside him closed the curtains and went on with the fight, pretending to take orders from the dead man and to transmit them to the captains.

The fate of Sebastian was sealed in that battle. Whether he lived or died, he disappeared on 5 August, 1578. One story was that after the battle of Alcaçer-el-Kebir, his body stripped and showing seven wounds was found in a heap of the slain; that it was taken to Fez and there buried; but was afterwards removed to Europe and found resting place in the Convent of Belen. Another story was that after a brilliant charge on his enemies he was taken in, but having been rescued by Lui de Brito he escaped unpursued. Certainly no one seemed to have seen the King killed, and it was strange that no part of his clothing or accoutrements was ever found. These were of great splendour, beauty and worth, and must have been easily traceable. There was a rumour that on the night following the battle some fugitives, amongst whom was one of commanding distinction, sought refuge at Arzilla.

Alcaçer-el-Kebir was known as the "Battle of the three Kings." All the principals engaged in it perished. Sebastian was killed or disappeared. Abd-el-Mulek died as we have seen, and Mohammed was drowned in trying to cross the river.

The dubiety of Sebastian's death gave rise in after years to several impostures.

The first began six years after Sebastian's successor—his uncle, Cardinal Henry—was placed on the throne. The impostor was known as the "King of Penamacor." The son of a potter at Alcobaca, he established himself at Albuquerque, within the Spanish borders, somewhat to the north of Badajos, and there gave himself out as "a survivor of the African Campaign." As usual the public went a little further and said openly that he was the missing Don Sebastian. At first he denied the soft impeachment, but later on the temptation became too great for him and he accepted it and set up in

Penamacor, where he became known as the "King of Penamacor." He was arrested and paraded through Lisbon, bareheaded, as if to let the public see that he in no way resembled the personality of Sebastian. He was sent to the galleys for life. But he must have escaped, for later on he appeared in Paris as Silvio Pellico, Duke of Normandy, and was accepted as such in many of the salons in the exclusive Faubourg St. Germain.

The second personator of Sebastian was one Matheus Alvares, who having failed to become a monk, a year later imitated the first impostor, and in 1585 set up a hermitage at Ericeira. He bore some resemblance to the late king in build, and in the strength of this he boldly gave himself out as "King Sebastian" and set out for Lisbon. But he was arrested by the way and entered as a prisoner. He was tried and executed with frightful accessories to the execution.

The third artist in this imposture appeared in 1594. He was a Spaniard from Madrigal in Old Castile—a cook, sixty years old (Sebastian would have been just forty if he had lived). When arrested he was given but short shrift and shared the same ghastly fate as his predecessor.

The fourth, and last, imposture was more serious. This time the personator began in Venice in 1598, calling himself "Knight of the Cross."

As twenty years had now elapsed since the disappearance of Sebastian, he would have changed much in appearance, so in one respect the personator had less to contend against. Moreover the scene of endeavour was this time laid in Venice, a place even more widely removed in the sixteenth century from Lisbon by circumstances than by geographical position. Again witnesses who could give testimony to the individuality of the missing King of twenty years ago were few and far between. But on the other hand the new impostor had new difficulties to contend against. Henry, the Cardinal, had only occupied the Portuguese throne two years, for in 1580 Philip II of Spain had united the two crowns, and had held the dual monarchy for eighteen years. He was a very different antagonist from any one that might be of purely Portuguese origin.

In the eyes of many of the people—like all the Latin races naturally superstitious—one circumstance powerfully upheld the impostor's claim. So long ago as 1587, Don John de Castro had made a seemingly prophetic statement that Sebastian was alive and would manifest himself in due time. His utterance was, like most such prophecies of the kind, "conducive to its own fulfilment;" there were many —and some of them powerful—who were willing at the start to back up any initiator of such a claim. In his time Sebastian had been used, so far as it was possible to use a man of his temperament and position, by the intriguers of the Catholic Church, and the present occasion lent itself to their still-existent aims. Rome was very powerful four centuries ago, and its legions of adherents bound in many ties, were scattered throughout the known world. Be sure these could and would aid in any movement or intrigue which could be useful to the Church.

"The Knight of the Cross"—who insinuated, though he did not state so, that he was a Royal person was arrested on the showing of the Spanish Ambassador. He was a born liar, with all the readiness which the carrying out of such an adventure as he had planned requires. Not only was he well posted in known facts, but he seemed to be actually proof against cross-examination. The story he told was that after the battle of Alcaçer-el-Kebir he with some others, had sought temporary refuge in Arzilla and in trying to make his way from there to the East Indies, he had got to "Prester John's" land—the semi-fabled Ethiopia of those days. From thence he had been turned back, and had, after many adventures and much wandering—in the course of which he had been bought and sold a dozen times or more, found his way, alone, to Venice. Amongst other statements he alleged that Sebastian's confessor had already recognised and acknowledged him; but he was doubtless ignorant, when he made the statement, that Padre Mauricio, Don Sebastian's confessor, fell with his king in 1578. Two things, one, a positive inference and the other negative, told against him. He only knew of such matters as had been made public in depositions, and *he did not know Portuguese.* The result of his first trial was that he was sent to prison for two years.

But those two years of prison improved his case immensely. In that time he learned the Portuguese language and many facts of history. One of the first to believe—or to allege belief, in his story, Fray Estevan de Sampayo, a Dominican monk, was in 1599, sent by the Venetian authorities to Portugal to obtain an accredited description of the personal marks of King Sebastian. He returned within a year with a list of sixteen personal marks—attested by an Apostolic notary. Strange to say the prisoner exhibited every one of them—a complete agreement which in itself gave rise to the new suspicion that the list had been made out by, or on behalf of, the prisoner. The proof however was accepted—for the time; and he was released on the 28th of July, 1600—but with the imperative, humiliating proviso that he was to quit Venice within four and twenty hours under penalty of being sent to the galleys. A number of his supporters, who met him before he went, found that he had in reality no sort of resemblance to Sebastian. Don John de Castro, who was amongst them, said that a great change in Sebastian seemed to have taken place. (He had prophesied and adhered to his prophecy.) He now described him as a man of medium height and powerful frame, with hair and beard of black or dark brown, and said he had completely lost his beauty. "What has become of my fairness?" the swarthy ex-prisoner used to say. He had eyes of uncertain colour, not large but sparkling; high cheek bones; long nose; thin lips with the "Hapsburg droop" in the lower one. He was short from the waist up. (Sebastian's doublet would fit no other person.) His right leg and arm were longer than the left, the legs being slightly bowed like Sebastian's. He had small feet with extraordinarily high insteps; and large hands. "In fine," Don John summed up illogically, "he is the self-same Sebastian—except for such differences as resulted from years and labours." Some other particulars he added which are in no way helpful to a conclusion.

The Impostor told his friends that he had in 1597, sent a messenger from Constantinople to Portugal—one Marco Tullio Catizzone—who had never returned. Thence he had travelled to Rome—where, when he was just on the eve of being presented to the Holy Father, he was robbed of all he had; thence to Verona and so on to Venice. After his expulsion from Venice he seems to have found his way to Leghorn and Florence, and thence on to Naples, where he was handed over to the jurisdiction of the Spanish Viceroy, the Count of Lemos, who had visited him in prison, and who well remembered King Sebastian whom he had seen when in a diplomatic mission. The Viceroy came to the conclusion that he bore no likeness at all to Sebastian, that he was ignorant of all save the well known historical facts that had been published, and that his speech was of "corrupt Portuguese mingled with tell-tale phrases of Calabrian dialect." Thereupon he took active steps against him. One witness who was produced, recognized in him the real Marco Tullio Catizzone, and Count de Lemos sent for his wife, mother-in-law and brother-in-law, all of whom he had deceived and deserted. His wife, Donna Paula of Messina, acknowledged him; and he confessed his crime. Condemned to the galleys for life, Marco Tullio, out of consideration of a possibility of an error of justice, was so far given indulgence by the authorities that he did not have to wear prison dress or labour at the oar. Many of his supporters, who still believed in him, tried to mitigate his lot and treated him as a companion; so that the hulk at San Lucar, at the mouth of the Guadalquiver became a minor centre of intrigue. But still he was not content, and adventuring further, he tried to get money from the wife of Medina-Sidonia then Governor of Andalusia. He was again arrested with some of his associates. Incriminating documents were found on him. He was racked and confessed all. And so in his real name and parentage, Marco Tullio, son of Ippolit Catizzone of Taverna, and of Petronia Cortes his wife, and husband of Paula Gallardetta was executed. He had, though of liberal education, never worked at any occupation or calling; but he had previously to his great fraud, personated other men —amongst them Don Diego of Arragon. On 23rd of September, 1603, he was dragged on a hurdle to the Square of San Lucar; his right hand was cut off and he was hanged. Five of his companions, including two priests, shared his fate.

But in a way he and the previous impostors had a sort of posthumous revenge, for Sebastian had now entered into the region of Romantic Belief. He was, like King Arthur, the ideal and the heart of a great myth. He became "The Hidden King" who would some day return to aid his nation in the hour of peril—the destined Ruler of the Fifth Monarchy, the founder of an universal Empire of Peace.

A hundred years ago, the custom in British theatres was to finish the evening's performance with a farce. On this occasion the tragedy had been finished two centuries before the "comic relief" came. The occasion was in the French occupation of Portugal in 1807. The strange belief in the Hidden King broke out afresh. A rigorous censorship of Sebastianist literature was without avail —even though its disseminators were condemned by the still-existing Inquisition. The old prophecy was renewed, with a local and personal application —Napoleon was to be destroyed in the Holy Week of 1808, by the waiting Sebastian, whose approach from his mysterious retreat was to be veiled with a thick fog. There were to be new portents; the sky was to be emblazoned with a cross of the Order of Aviz, and on March 19th a full moon was to occur during the last quarter. All these things were foretold in an *egg,* afterwards sent by Junot to the National Museum. The general attitude of the French people towards the subject was illustrated by a remark in an ironical manner of one writer: "what can be looked for from a people, one half of whom await the Messiah, the other half Don Sebastian?" The authority on the subject of King Sebastian, M. d'Antas, relates that as late as 1838, after the crushing of a Sebastianist insurrection in Brazil certain still believing Sebastianists were to be seen along the coast peering through the fog for the sails of the mythical ship which was to bring to them the Hidden King who was then to reveal himself.

C. "STEFAN MALI"

THE FALSE CZAR

STEFAN MALI (Stephen the Little) was an impostor who passed himself off in Montenegro as the Czar Peter III of Russia, who was supposed to have been murdered in 1762. He appeared in the Bocche di Cattaro in 1767. No one seemed to know him or to doubt him; indeed after he had put forth his story he did not escape identification. One witness who had accompanied a state visit to Russia averred that he recognized the features of the Czar whom he had seen in St. Petersburg. Like all adventurers Stefan Mali had good personal resources. An adventurer, and especially an adventurer who is also an impostor, must be an opportunist; and an opportunist must be able to move in any direction at any time; therefore he must be always ready for any emergency. The time, the place, and the circumstances largely favoured the impostor in this case. It is perhaps but fair to credit him with foreknowledge, intention, and understanding of all that he did. In after years he justified himself in this respect and showed distinctly that he was a man of brains and capable of using them. He was no doubt not only able to sustain at the start his alleged personality, but also to act under new conditions and in new circumstances as they developed themselves, as a man of Czar Peter's character and acquired knowledge might have done. Cesare Augusto Levi, who is the authority on this subject, says, in his work *"Venezia e il Montenegro"*: "He was of fine presence and well proportioned form and of noble ways. He was so eloquent that he exercised with mere words a power not only on the multitude but also on the higher classes. . . . He must certainly have been in St. Petersburg before he scaled Montenegro; and have known the true Peter III, for he imitated his voice and his gestures—to the illusionment of the Montenegrins. There is no certainty of such a thing, but he must, in the belief of the Vladika Sava have been a descendant of Stefano Czernovich who reigned after Giorgio IV."

At that time Montenegro was ruled by Vladika Sava, who having spent some twenty years in monastic life, was unfitted for the government of a turbulent nation always harassed by the Turks and always engaged in a struggle for bare existence. The people of such a nation naturally wanted a strong ruler, and as they were discontented under the sway of Sava the recognition of Stefan Mali was almost a foregone conclusion. He told a wonderful story of his adventures since his reported death—a story naturally interesting to such an adventurous people; and as he stated his intention of never returning to Russia, they were glad to add such a new ally to their fighting force for the maintenance of their independence. As the will of the people was for the new-comer, the Vladika readily consented to confine himself to his spiritual functions and to allow Stefan to govern. The Vladika of Montenegro held a strange office—one which combined the functions of priest and generalissimo —so that the new division of the labour of ruling was rather welcome than otherwise to the people of a nation where no man ever goes without arms. Stephen—as he now was—governed well. He devoted himself fearlessly to the punishment of ill-doing, and early in his reign had men shot for theft. He established Courts of Justice and tried to further means of communication throughout the little kingdom, which, is, after all, little more than a bare rock. He even so far impinged on Sava's sacred office as to prohibit Sunday labour. In fact his labours so much improved the outlook of the Montenegrins that the result brought trouble on himself as well as on the nation in general. Hitherto, whatever foreign nations may have believed as to the authenticity of Stephen's claim, they had deliberately closed their eyes to his new existence, so long as under his rule the little nation of Montenegro did not become a more dangerous enemy to all or any of them.

But the nations interested grew anxious at the

forward movement in Montenegro. Venice, then the possessor of Dalmatia, was alarmed, and Turkey regarded the new ruler as an indirect agent of Russia. Together they declared war. This was the moment when Fate declared that the Pretender should show his latent weakness of character. The Montenegrins are naturally so brave that cowardice is unknown amongst them; but Stephen did not dare to face the Turkish army, which attacked Montenegro on all the land sides. But the Montenegrins fought on till a chance came to them after many months of waiting in the shape of a fearful storm which desolated their enemies' Camp. By a sudden swoop on the camp they seized much ammunition of which they were sadly in want and by the aid of which they gained delivery from their foes. The Russian government seemed then to wake up to the importance of the situation, and, after sending the Montenegrins much help in the shape of war material, asked them to join again in the war against the Turks. The Empress Catherine in addition to this request, sent another letter denouncing Stephen as an impostor. He admitted the charge and was put in prison. But in the impending war a strong man was wanted at the head of affairs; and Sava, who now had the mundane side of his dual office once more thrust again upon him, was a weak one. The situation was saved by Prince George Dolgourouki, the representative of the Empress Catherine, who, with statesmanlike acumen, saw that such a desperate need required an exceptional remedy. He recognized the false Czar as Regent. Stephen Mali, thus restored to power under such powerful auspices, once more governed Montenegro until 1774, when he was murdered by the Greek player Casamugna—by order, it is said, of the Pasha of Scutari, Kara Mahmound.

By the irony of Fate this was exactly the way in which the real Czar, whose personality he had assumed, had died some dozen years before.

This impostor was perhaps the only one who in the history of nations prospered finally in his fraud. But as may be seen he was possessed of higher gifts than most of his kind; he was equal to the emergencies which presented themselves—and circumstances favoured him, rarely.

D. THE FALSE DAUPHINS

ON 21 January, 1793, Louis XVI of France was beheaded in the Place de la Revolution, formerly Place de Louis Quinze. From the moment his head fell, his only son the Dauphin became by all constitutional usage, his successor, Louis XVII. True the child-king was in the hands of his enemies; but what mattered that to believers in the "Divine Right." What mattered it either that he was at that moment in the prison of the Temple, where he had languished since August 13, 1792, already consecrated to destruction, in one form or another. He was then under eight years of age, and so an easy victim. His gaoler, one Simon, had already been instructed to bring him up as a "sansculotte." In the furtherance of this dreadful ordinance he was taught to drink and swear and to take a part in the unrighteous songs and ceremonies of the Reign of Terror. Under such conditions no one can be sorry that death came to his relief. This was in June, 1795—he being then in his eleventh year. In the stress and turmoil of such an overwhelming cataclysm as the Revolution, but little notice was taken of a death which, under other circumstances, would undoubtedly have been of international interest if not of importance. But by this time the death of any one, so long as it was by violence, was too common a matter to cause concern to others. The Terror had practically glutted the lust for blood. Under such conditions but little weight was placed on the accuracy of records; and to this day there survive practical inconveniences and difficulties in daily life from the then disruption of ordered ways. The origin of such frauds or means of fraud as are now before us is in uncertainty. Shakespeare says:

> "How oft the sight of means to do ill deeds
> Makes ill deeds done."

The true or natural criminal is essentially an opportunist. The intention of crime, even if it be only a desire to follow the line of least resistance, is a permanent factor in such lives, but the direction, the mechanism, and the scope of the crime are largely the result of the possibilities which open and develop themselves from a fore-ordered condition of things.

Here then was the opening which presented itself at the end of the eighteenth century. France was in a state of social chaos. The fountains of the deep were stirred, and no human intelligence could do more than guess at what might result from any individual effort of self-advancement. The public conscience was debauched, and for all practical purposes the end justified the means. It was an age of desperate adventure, of reckless enterprise, of unscrupulous methods. The Royalty of France was overthrown—in abeyance till at least such a time as some Colossus of brains or energy, or good fortune, should set it up again. The hopes of a great nation of return to a settled order of things through constitutional and historical channels were centred in the succession to the Crown. And through the violence of the upheaval any issue was possible. The state of affairs just before the death of Louis XVII gave a chance of success to any desperate fraud. The old King was dead, the new King was a child and in the hands of his bitterest enemies. Even if anyone had cared to vindicate his rights there seemed at present no way of accomplishing this object. To any reckless and unscrupulous adventurer here was an unique chance. Here was a kingship going: a daring hand might grasp the crown which rested in so perilous a manner on the head of a baby. Moreover the events of the last fifteen years of the century had not only begotten daring which depended on promptness, but had taught and fostered desperation. It is a wonder to us who look back on that time through the safety-giving mist of a century, not that there was any attempt to get a crown, if only by theft, but that there were not a hundred attempts made for each one that history has recorded.

As a matter of fact, there were seven attempts made to personate the dead Dauphin, son of Louis XVI, that "son of St. Louis," who, in obedience to Abbé Edgworth's direction to "ascend to heaven," went somewhere where it is difficult—or perhaps inexpedient—to follow him.

The first pretender appears to have been one Jean Marie Hervagault, son of a tailor. His qualification for the pretence appears to have been but a slender one, that of having been born in 1781, only about three years before the Dauphin. This, taken by itself, would seem to be but a poor equipment for such a crime; but in comparison with some of the later claimants it was not without reason of approximate possibility as far as date was concerned. It was not this criminal's first attempt at imposture, for he had already pretended to be a son of la Vaucelle of Longueville and of the Duc d'Ursef. Having been arrested at Hottot as a vagabond, he was taken to Cherburg, where he was claimed by his father. When claiming to be, like the old man in Mark Twain's inimitable *Huckleberry Finn*, "the late Dauphin," his story was that he had as a child been carried from the prison of the Temple in a basket of linen. In 1799 he was imprisoned at Chalons-sur-Marne for a month. He was, however, so far successful in his imposture as Louis XVII, that after some adventures he actually achieved a good following—chiefly of the landed interest and clerics.

He was condemned to two years' imprisonment at Vitry, and afterwards to a term of twice that duration, during which he died, in 1812.

The second and third aspirants to the honour of the vacant crown were inconspicuous persons possessing neither personal qualification nor apparent claim of any sort except that of a desire for acquisition. One was Persat, an old soldier; the other, Fontolive, a bricklayer. The pretence of either of these men would have been entirely ridiculous but for its entirely tragic consequences. There is short shrift for the unsuccessful impostor of royalty—even in an age of fluctuation between rebellion and anarchy.

The fourth pretender was at least a better workman at crime than his predecessors. This was Mathurin Brunneau—ostensibly a shoemaker but in reality a vagabond peasant from Vezins, in the department of Maine-et-Loire. He was a born criminal as was shown by his early record. When only eleven years of age he claimed to be the son of the lord of the village, Baron de Vezins. He obtained the sympathy of the Countess de Turpin de Crisse, who seemed to have compassion for the boy. Even when the fraud of his parentage was found out she took him back into her household—but amongst the servants. After this his life became one of adventure. When he was fifteen he made a tour through France. In 1803 he was put in the House of Correction at St. Denis. In 1805 he enlisted as a gunner. In 1815 he re-appeared with an American passport bearing the name of Charles de Navarre. His more ambitious attempt at personation in 1817, was not in the long run successful. He claimed his rights, as "Dauphin" Bourbon under Louis XVIII, was arrested at St. Malo, and confined at Bicêtre. He got round him a gang of persons of evil life, as shown by their various records. One was a false priest, another a prisoner for embezzlement, another an ex-bailiff who was also a forger, another a deserter; with the usual criminal concomitant of women, dishonoured clergy and such like. At Rouen he was sentenced to pay a fine of three thousand francs in addition to imprisonment for seven years. He died in prison.

The imposture regarding the Dauphin was like a torch-race—so soon as the lighted torch fell from the hand of one runner it was lifted by him who followed. Brunneau, having disappeared into the prison at Rouen, was succeeded by Henri Herbert who made a dramatic appearance in Austria in 1818. At the Court in Mantone, the scene of his appearance, he gave the name of Louis Charles de Bourbon, Duc de Normandie. His account of himself, given in his book published in 1831, and republished—with enlargements, by Chevalier del Corso in 1850, is without any respect at all for the credulity of his readers.

The story tells how an alleged doctor, one answering to the not common name of Jenais-Ojardias, some time before the death of the Dauphin had had made a toy horse of sufficient size to contain the baby king, the opening to the interior of which was hidden by the saddle-cloth. The wife of the gaoler Simon, helped in the plot, the carrying out of which was attempted early in 1794. Another child about the Dauphin's size, dying or marked for death by fatal disease, was drugged and hidden in the interior. When the toy horse was placed in the Dauphin's cell the children were exchanged, the little king having also been drugged for the purpose. It would almost seem that the narrator here either lost his head or was seized with a violent *cacoethes scribendi,* for he most unnecessarily again lugs in the episode adapted from Trojan history. The worthy doctor of the double name had another horse manufactured, this time of life size. Into the alleged entrails of this animal, which was harnessed with three real horses as one of a team of four, the Dauphin, once more drugged, was concealed. He was borne to refuge in Belgium, where he was placed under the protection of the Prince de Condé. By this protector he was, according to his story, sent to General Kléber who took him to Egypt as his nephew under the name of Monsieur Louis. After the battle of Marengo in 1800, he returned to France, where he confided his secret to Lucien Bonaparte and to Fouché (the Minister of Police), who got him introduced to the Empress Josephine, who recognised him by a scar over his right eye. In 1804 (still according to his story), he embarked for America and got away to the banks of the Amazon, where amid the burning deserts (as he put it) he had adventures capable of consuming lesser romancists with envy. Some of these adventures were amongst a tribe called "the Mamelucks"—which name was at least reminiscent of his alleged Egyptian experiences. From the burning deserts on the banks of the Amazon he found his way to Brazil, where a certain "Don Juan," late of Portugal and at that time Regent of Brazil, gave him asylum.

Leaving the hospitable home of Don Juan, he returned to Paris in 1815. Here Condé introduced him to the Duchesse d'Angoulême (his sister!) and according to his own naïve statement "the Princess was greatly surprised," as indeed she might well have been—quite as much as the witch of Endor was by the appearance of Samuel. Having been repulsed by his (alleged) sister, the alleged king made a little excursion, embracing in its erratic course Rhodes, England, Africa, Egypt, Asia Minor, Greece, and Italy. When in Austria he met Silvio Pellico in prison. Having spent some years himself in prison in the same country, he went to Switzerland. Leaving Geneva in 1826, he entered France, under the name of Herbert. He was in Paris the following year under the name of "Colonel Gustave," and forthwith revived his fraud of being "the late Dauphin." In 1828, he appealed to the Chamber of Peers. To this appeal he appears to have received no direct reply; but apropos of it, Baron Mounier made a proposition to the Chamber that in future no such application should be received unless properly signed and attested and presented by a member of the Chamber. He gathered round him some dupes who believed in him. To these he told a number of strange lies based on some form of perverted truth, but always taking care that those of whom he spoke were already dead. Amongst them was the wife of Simon, who had died in 1819. Desault, the surgeon, who had medical care of Louis XVII, and who died in 1795, the ex-Empress Josephine, who died in 1814, General Pichegru, who died in 1804, and the Duc de Bourbon (Prince de Condé) who died in 1818. In the course of his citation of the above names, he plays havoc with generally accepted history—Desault according to him did not die naturally but was poisoned. Josephine died simply because she knew the secret of the young King's escape. Pichegru died from a similar cause and not by suicide. Fualdes was assassinated, but it was because he knew the fatal secret. With regard to one of his dead witnesses whose name was Thomas-Ignace-Martin de Gallardon, there is a rigmarole which would not be accepted in the nursery of an idiot asylum. There is a mixture of Pagan mythology and Christian hagiology which would have been condemned by Ananias himself. In one passage he talks of seeing suddenly before him—he could not tell (naturally enough) whence he came—a sort of angel who had wings, a long coat and a *high hat*. This supernatural person ordered the narrator to tell the King that he was in danger, and the only way to avoid it was to have a good police and to keep the Sabbath. Having given his message the visitant rose in the air and disappeared. Later on the suggested angel told him to communicate with the Duc Decazes. The Duke naturally, and wisely enough, handed the credulous peasant over to the care of a doctor. Martin himself died, presumably by assassination, in 1834.

The Revolution of 1830 awoke the pretensions of Herbert, who now appeared as the Baron de Richemont, and wrote to the Duchesse d'Angoulême, his (supposed) sister, putting on her the blame of all his troubles. But the consequences of this effort were disastrous to him. He was arrested in August, 1833. After hearing many witnesses the Court condemned him to imprisonment for twelve years. He was arraigned under the name of "Ethelbert Louis-Hector-Alfred," calling himself the "Baron de Richmont." He escaped from Clairvaux, whither he had been transferred from Saint-Pélagie, in 1835. In 1843 and 1846 he published his memoirs—enlarged but omitting some of his earlier assertions, which had been disproved. He returned to France after the amnesty of 1840. In 1848 he appealed—unheeded—to the National Assembly. He died in 1855 at Gleyze.

The sixth "Late Dauphin" was a Polish Jew called Naundorf—an impudent impostor not even seeming suitably prepared by time for the part which he had thus voluntarily undertaken, having been born in 1775, and thus having been as old at the birth of the Dauphin as the latter was when he died. This individual had appeared in Berlin in 1810, and was married in Spandau eight years later. He had been punished for incendiarism in 1824, and later got three years' imprisonment at Brandenburg for coining. He may be considered as a fairly good all-round—if unsuccessful—criminal. In England he was imprisoned for debt. He died in Delft in 1845.

The last attempt at impersonating Louis XVII, the seventh, afforded what might in theatrical parlance be called the "comic relief" of the whole series, both as regards means and results. This time the claimant to the Kingship of France was none other than a half-bred Iroquois, one called Eleazar, who appeared to be the ninth son of Thomas Williams, otherwise Thorakwaneken, and an Indian woman, Mary Ann Konwatewentala. This lady, who spoke only Iroquois, said at the opportune time she was *not* the mother of Lazar (Iroquois for Eleazar). She made her mark as she could not write.

Eleazar had been almost an idiot till the age of thirteen; but, being struck on the head by a stone, recovered his memory and intelligence. He said he remembered sitting on the knees of a beautiful lady who wore a rich dress with a train. He also remembered seeing in his childhood a terrible person; shewn the picture of Simon he recognised him with terror. He learned English but imperfectly, became a Protestant and a missionary and married. His profile was something like that of the typical Bourbon. In 1841, the Prince de Joinville, seeing him on his travels in the United States, told him (according to Eleazar's account) that he was the son of a king, and got him to sign and seal a parchment, already prepared, the same being a solemn abdication of the Crown of France in favour of Louis Philippe, made by Charles Louis, son of Louis XVI, also styled Louis XVII King of France and Navarre. The seal used was the seal of France, the one used by the old Monarchy. The "poor Indian with untutored mind" made with charming diffidence the saving clause regarding the seal,—"if I am not mistaken." Of course there was in the abdication a clause regarding the payment of a sum of money "which would enable me to live in great luxury in this country or in France as I might choose." The Reverend Eleazar, despite his natural disadvantages and difficulties, was more fortunate than his fellow claimants inasmuch as the time of his imposture was more propitious. Louis Philippe, who was always anxious to lessen the danger to his tottering throne, made a settlement on him from his Civil List, and the "subsequent proceedings interested him no more."

Altogether the Louis XVII impostures extended over a period of some sixty years, beginning with Hervagault's pretence soon after the death of the Dauphin, and closing at Gleyze with the death of Henri Herbert, the alleged Baron de Richmont who appeared as the alleged Duc de Normandie.

E. PRINCESS OLIVE

THE story of Mrs. Olive Serres, as nature made it, was one thing; it was quite another as she made it for herself. The result, before the story was completely told, was a third; and, compared with the other, one of transcendent importance. Altogether her efforts, whatsoever they were and crowned never so effectively, showed a triumph in its way of the thaumaturgic art of lying; but like all structures built on sand it collapsed eventually. In the plain version—nature's—the facts were simply as follows. She, and a brother of no importance, were the children of a house painter living in Warwick, one Robert Wilmot, and of Anna Maria his wife. Having been born in 1772 she was under age when in 1791 she was married, the ceremony therefore requiring licence supported by bond and affidavit. Her husband was John Thomas Serres who ten years later was appointed marine painter to King George III. Mr. and Mrs. Serres were separated in 1804 after the birth of two daughters, the elder of whom, born in 1797, became in 1822 the wife of Antony Thomas Ryves a portrait painter—whom she divorced in 1847. Mrs. A. T.

Ryves twelve years later filed a petition praying that the marriage of her mother, made in 1791, might be declared valid and she herself the legitimate issue of that marriage. The case was heard in 1861, Mrs. Ryves conducting it in person. Having produced sufficient evidence of the marriage and the birth, and there being no opposition, the Court almost as a matter of course pronounced the decree asked for. In this case no complications in the way of birth or marriage of Mrs. Serres were touched on.

Robert Wilmot, the house-painter, had an elder brother James who became a Fellow of Trinity College, Oxford, and went into the Church, taking his degree of Doctor of Divinity. Through his College he was presented in 1781 to the living of Barton-on-the-heath, Warwickshire. The Statutes of his College contained a prohibition against marriage whilst a Fellow. James Wilmot D. D. died in 1807 leaving his property between the two children of Robert, after life-use by his brother. James and Robert Wilmot had a sister Olive, who was born in 1728 and married in 1754 to William Payne with issue one daughter, Olivia, born in 1759. Robert Wilmot died in 1812.

Out of these rough materials Mrs. Olive Serres set herself in due course to construct and carry out, as time and opportunity allowed, and as occasions presented themselves and developed, a fraudulent romance in real life and action. She was, however,

OLIVIA SERRES

a very clever woman and in certain ways—as was afterwards proved by her literary and artistic work —well dowered by nature for the task—crooked though it was—which she set for herself. Her ability was shown not only by what she could do and did at this time of her life, but by the manner in which she developed her natural gifts as time went on. In the sum of her working life, in which the perspective of days becomes merged in that of years, she touched on many subjects, not always of an ordinary kind, which shewed often that she was of conspicuous ability, having become accomplished in several branches of art. She was a painter of sufficient merit to have exhibited her work in the Royal Academy in 1794 and to be appointed landscape-painter to the Prince of Wales in 1806. She was a novelist, a press writer, an occasional poet and in many ways of a ready pen. She was skilled in some forms of occultism, and could cast horoscopes; she wrote, in addition to a pamphlet on the same subject, a book on the writings of Junius, claiming to have discovered the identity of the author—none other than James Wilmot D. D. She wrote learnedly on disguised handwriting. In fact she touched on the many phases of literary effort which come within the scope of those who live by the work of their brains. Perhaps, indeed, it was her facility as a writer that helped to lead her astray; for in her practical draughtsmanship and in her brain teeming with romantic ideas she found a means of availing herself of opportunities suggested by her reckless ambition. Doubtless the cramped and unpoetic life of her humble condition in the house-painter's home in Warwick made her fret and chafe under its natural restraint. But when she saw her way to an effective scheme of enlarging her self-importance she acted with extraordinary daring and resource. As is usual with such natures, when moral restraints have been abandoned, the pendulum swung to its opposite. As she had been lowly she determined to be proud; and having fixed on her objective began to elaborate a consistent scheme, utilising the facts of her own surroundings as the foundation of her imposture. She probably realised early that there must be a base somewhere, and so proceeded to manufacture or arrange for herself a new identity into which the demonstrable facts of her actual life could be wrought. At the same time she manifestly realised that in a similar way fact and intention must be interwoven throughout the whole of her contemplated creation. Accordingly she created for herself a new *milieu* which she supported by forged documents of so clever a conceit and such excellent workmanship, that they misled all who investigated them, until they came within the purview of the great lawyers of the day whose knowledge, logical power, skill and determination were arrayed against her. By a sort of intellectual metabolism she changed the identities and conditions of her own relations whom I have mentioned, always taking care that her story held together in essential possibilities, and making use of the abnormalities of those whose prototypes she introduced into fictional life.

The changes made in her world of new conditions were mainly as follows: Her uncle, the Reverend James, who as a man of learning and dignity was accustomed to high-class society, and as a preacher of eminence occasionally in touch with Crown and Court, became her father; and she herself the child of a secret marriage with a great lady whose personal rank and condition would reflect importance on her daughter. But proof, or alleged proof, of some kind would be necessary and there were too many persons at present living whose testimony would be available for her undoing. So her uncle James shifted his place and became her grandfather. To this the circumstances of his earlier life gave credibility in two ways; firstly because they allowed of his having made a secret marriage, since he was forbidden to marry by the statutes of his college, and secondly because they gave a reasonable excuse for concealing his marriage and the birth of a child, publicity regarding which would have cost him his livelihood.

At this point the story began to grow logically, and the whole scheme to expand cohesively. Her genius as a writer of fiction was being proved; and with the strengthening of the intellectual nature came the atrophy of the moral. She began to look higher; and the seeds of imagination took root in her vanity till the madness latent in her nature turned wishes into beliefs and beliefs into facts. As she was imagining on her own behoof, why not imagine beneficially? This all took time, so that when she was well prepared for her venture things had moved on in the nation and the world as well as in her fictitious romance. Manifestly she could not make a start on her venture until the possibility vanished of witnesses from the inner circle of her own family being brought against her; so that she could not safely begin machinations for some time. She determined however to be ready when occasion should serve. In the meantime she had to lead two lives. Outwardly she was Olive Serres, daughter of Robert Wilmot born in 1772 and married in 1791, and mother of two daughters. Inwardly she was the same woman with the same birth, marriage and motherhood, but of different descent being (imaginatively) grand-daughter of her (real) uncle the Rev. James Wilmot D. D. The gaps in the imaginary descent having been thus filled up as made and provided in her own mind, she felt more safe. Her uncle—so ran her fiction—had early in his college life met and become friends with Count Stanislaus Poniatowski who later became by election King of Poland. Count Poniatowski had a sister—whom the ingenious Olive dubbed "Princess of Poland"—who became the wife of her uncle (now her grandfather) James. To them was born, in 1750, a daughter Olive, the marriage being kept secret for family reasons, and the child for the same reason being passed off as the offspring of Robert the housepainter. This child Olive, according to the fiction, met His Royal Highness Henry Frederick, Duke of Cumberland, brother of the King, George III. They fell in love with each other and were privately married—by the Rev. James Wilmot D. D.—on 4 March 1767. They had issue one daughter, Olive, born at Warwick 3 April 1772. After living with her for four years the Duke of Cumberland deserted his wife, who was then pregnant, and in 1771 married—bigamously, it was alleged—Lady Anne Horton, sister of Colonel Luttrell, daughter of Lord Irnham, and widow of Andrew Horton of Catton, Derbyshire. The (alleged) Royal Duchess died in France in 1774, and the Duke in 1790.

Thus fact and fiction were arrayed together in a very cunning way. The birth of Olive Wilmot (afterwards Serres) in 1772 was proved by a genuine registry. Likewise that of her daughter Mrs. Ryves. For all the rest the certificates were forged. Moreover there was proof of another Olive Wilmot whose existence, supported by genuine registration, might avert suspicion; since it would be difficult to prove after a lapse of time that the Olive Wilmot born at Warwick in 1772 daughter of Robert (the house-painter), was not the granddaughter of James (the Doctor of Divinity). In case of necessity the real date (1759) of the birth of Olive Wilmot sister of the Rev. James could easily be altered to the fictitious date of the birth of "Princess" Olive born 1750.

It was only in 1817 that Mrs. Serres began to take active measures for carrying her imposture into action; and in the process she made some tentative efforts which afterwards made difficulty for her. At first she sent out a story, through a memorial to George III, that she was daughter of the Duke of Cumberland by Mrs. Payne, wife of Captain Payne and sister of James Wilmot D. D. This she amended later in the same year by alleging that she was a natural daughter of the Duke by the sister of Doctor Wilmot, whom he had seduced under promise of marriage. It was not till after the deaths of George III and the Duke of Kent in 1820, that the story took its third and final form.

It should be noticed that care was taken not to clash with laws already in existence or to run counter to generally received facts. In 1772 was passed the Royal Marriage Act (12 George III Cap. 11) which nullified any marriage contracted with anyone in the succession to the Crown to which the Monarch had not given his sanction. Therefore Mrs. Serres had fixed the (alleged) marriage of (the alleged) Olive Wilmot with the Duke of Cumberland as in 1767—five years earlier—so that the Act could not be brought forward as a bar to its validity. Up to 1772 such marriages could take place legally. Indeed there was actually a case in existence—the Duke of Gloucester (another brother of the King) having married the dowager Countess of Waldegrave. It was of common repute that this marriage was the motive of the King's resolve to have the Royal Marriage Act added to the Statute book. At the main trial it was alleged by Counsel, in making the petitioner's claim, that the King (George III) was aware of the Duke of Cumberland's marriage with Olive Wilmot, although it was not known to the public, and that when he heard of his marriage with Lady Anne Horton he was very angry and would not allow them to come to Court.

The various allegations of Mrs. Serres as to her mother's marriage were not treated seriously for a long time but they were so persisted in that it became necessary to have some denial in evidence. Accordingly a law-case was entered. One which became a *cause célèbre*. It began in 1866—just about a hundred years from the time of the alleged marriage. With such a long gap the difficulties of disproving Mrs. Serres' allegations were much increased. But there was no help for it; reasons of State forbade the acceptance or even the doubt of such a claim. The really important point was that if by any chance the claimant should win, the Succession would be endangered.

The presiding judge was the Lord Chief Justice, Lord Cockburn. With him sat Lord Chief Baron Pollock and the Judge Ordinary Sir James Wilde. There was a special jury. The case took the form of one in the English Probate Court made under the "Legitimacy Declaration Act." In this case, Mrs. Ryves, daughter of Mrs. Serres, was the petitioner. Associated with her in the claim was her son, who, however, is of no interest in the matter and need not be considered. The petition stated that Mrs. Ryves was the legitimate daughter of one John Thomas Serres and Olive his wife, the said Olive being, whilst living, a natural-born subject and the legitimate daughter of Henry Frederick, Duke of Cumberland and Olive Wilmot, his wife. That the said Olive Wilmot, born in 1750, was lawfully married to His Royal Highness Henry Frederick, Duke of Cumberland, fourth son of Frederick Prince of Wales (thus being grandson of George II and brother of King George III), on 4 March 1767, at the house of Thomas, Lord Archer, in Grosvenor Square, London, the marriage being performed by the Rev. James Wilmot D. D., father of the said Olive Wilmot. That a child, Olive, was born to them on 3 April 1772, who in 1791 was married to John Thomas Serres. And so on in accordance with the (alleged) facts above given.

The strange position was that even if the petitioner should win her main case she would prove her own illegitimacy. For granting that the alleged Olive Serres should have been legally married to the Duke of Cumberland, the Royal Marriage Act, passed five years later, forbade the union of the child of such a marriage, except with the sanction of the reigning monarch.

In the making of the claim of Mrs. Ryves a grave matter appeared—one which rendered it absolutely necessary that the case should be heard in the most formal and adequate way and settled once for all. The matter was one affecting the legality of the marriage of George III, and so touching the legitimacy of his son afterwards George IV, his son afterwards William IV and his son the Duke of Kent, father of Queen Victoria—and so debarring them and all their descendants from the Crown of England. The points of contact were in documents insidiously though not overtly produced and the preparation of which showed much constructive skill in the world of fiction. Amongst the many documents put in evidence by the Counsel for Mrs. Ryves were two certificates of the (alleged) marriage between Olive Wilmot and the Duke of Cumberland. On the back of each of these alleged certificates was written what purported to be a certificate of the marriage of George III to Hannah Lightfoot performed in 1759 by J. Wilmot. The wording of the documents varied slightly.

It was thus that the claim of Mrs. Ryves and her son became linked up with the present and future destinies of England. These alleged documents too, brought the Attorney General upon the scene. There were two reasons for this. Firstly the action had to be taken against the Crown in the matter of form; secondly in such a case with the possibility of such vast issues it was absolutely necessary that every position should be carefully guarded, every allegation jealously examined. In each case the Attorney General was the proper official to act.

The Case of the Petitioners was prepared with extraordinary care. There were amongst the documents produced, numbering over seventy, some containing amongst them forty-three signatures of Dr. Wilmot, sixteen of Lord Chatham, twelve of Mr. Dunning (afterwards the 1st Baron Ashburton), twelve of George III, thirty-two of Lord Warwick and eighteen of H.R.H., the Duke of Kent, the father of Queen Victoria. Their counsel stated that although these documents had been repeatedly brought to the notice of the successive Ministers of the Crown, it had never been suggested until that day that they were forgeries. This latter statement was traversed in Court by the Lord Chief Baron, who called attention to a debate on the subject in the House of Commons in which they were denounced as forgeries.

In addition to those documents already quoted were the following certificates:

"The marriage of these parties was this day duly solemnized at Kew Chapel, according to the rites and ceremonies of the Church of England, by myself.

"J. Wilmot."

"George P."
"Hannah."

Witness to this marriage

"W. Pitt."
"Anne Taylor."

May 27, 1759.

April 17, 1759

"This is to Certify that the marriage o these parties (George, Prince of Wales, to Hannah Lightfoot) was duly solemnized this day, according to the rites and ceremonies of the Church of England, at their residence at Peckham, by myself.

"J. Wilmot."

"George Guelph."
"Hannah Lightfoot."

Witness to the marriage of these parties,—

"William Pitt."
"Anne Taylor."

"I hereby Certify that George, Prince of Wales, married Hannah Wheeler *alias* Lightfoot, April 17, 1759, but from finding the latter to be her right name I solemnized the union of the said parties a second time May the 27th, 1759, as the Certificate affixed to this paper will confirm.

"J. Wilmot.
Witness (Torn)

The case for the Crown was strongly supported. Not only did the Attorney-General, Sir Roundell Palmer (afterwards Lord Chancellor and First Earl of Selborne) appear himself, but he was supported by the Solicitor-General, the Queen's Advocate, Mr. Hannen and Mr. R. Bourke. The Attorney-General made the defence himself. At the outset it was difficult to know where to begin, for everywhere undoubted and unchallenged facts were interwoven with the structure of the case; and of all the weaknesses and foibles of the important persons mentioned, full advantage was taken. The marriage of the Duke of Gloucester to Lady Waldegrave had made him unpopular in every way, and he was at the time a *persona ingrata* at Court. There had been rumours of scandal about the King (when Prince of Wales) and the "Fair Quaker," Hannah Lightfoot. The anonymity of the author of the celebrated "Letters of Junius," which attacked the King so unmercifully, lent plausibility to any story which might account for it. The case of Mrs. Ryves, tried in 1861, in which her own legitimacy had been proved and in which indisputable documents had been used, was taken as a proof of her *bona fides*.

Mrs. Ryves herself was in the box for nearly the whole of three days, during which she bore herself firmly, refusing even to sit down when the presiding judge courteously extended that privilege to her. She was then, by her own statement, over seventy years of age. In the course of her evidence a Memorial to George IV was produced, written by her mother, Mrs. Serres, in which the word offspring was spelled "orfspring"; in commenting on which the Attorney-General produced a congratulatory Ode to the Prince Regent on his birthday in 1812, by the same author, in which occurred the line:

"Hail valued heir orfspring of Heaven's smile."

Similar eccentric orthography was found in other autograph papers of Mrs. Serres.

The Attorney-General, in opposing the claim, alleged that the whole story of the Duke of Cumberland's marriage to Olive Wilmot was a concoction from beginning to end, and said that the mere statement of the Petitioner's case was sufficient to stamp its true character. That its folly and absurdity were equal to its audacity; in every stage it exposed itself to conviction by the simplest tests. He added that the Petitioner might have dwelt so long upon documents produced and fabricated by others, that, with her memory impaired by old age, the principle of veracity might have been poisoned, and the offices of imagination and memory confounded to such an extent that she really believed that things had been done and said in her presence which were in fact entirely imaginary. No part of her story was corroborated by a single authentic document, or by a single extrinsic fact. The forgery, falsehood and fraud of the case were proved in many ways. The explanations were as false and feeble as the story itself. "I cannot of course," he said, "lay bare the whole history of the concoction of these extraordinary documents, but there are circumstances which indicate that they were concocted by Mrs. Serres herself."

Having commented on some other matters spoken of, but regarding which no evidence was adduced, he proceeded to speak of the alleged wife of Joseph Wilmot D. D., the Polish Princess, sister of Count Poniatowski, afterwards elected King of Poland (1764), who was the mother of his charming daughter, Olive. "The truth is," said Sir Roundell, "that both the Polish Princess and the charming daughter were pure myths; no such persons ever existed—they were as entirely creatures of the imagination as Shakespeare's Ferdinand and Miranda."

As to the documents produced by the Petitioners he remarked:

"What sort of documents were those which were produced? The internal evidence proved that they were the most ridiculous, absurd, preposterous series of forgeries that the perverted ingenuity of man ever invented . . . they were all written on little scraps and slips of paper, such as no human being would ever have used for the purpose of recording transactions of this kind, and it would be proved that in every one of these pieces of paper the watermark of date was wanting."

This was but a new variant of the remark made by the Lord Chief Justice, just after the putting-in of the alleged marriage Certificate of the Prince of Wales and Hannah Lightfoot:

"The Court is, as I understand, asked solemnly to declare, on the strength of two certificates, coming I know not whence, written on two scraps of paper, that the marriage, the only marriage of George III which the world believes to have taken place, between His Majesty and Queen Charlotte, was an invalid marriage, and consequently that all the Sovereigns who have sat on the throne since his death, including Her present Majesty, were not entitled to sit on the throne. That is the conclusion which the Court is asked to come to upon these two rubbishy pieces of paper, one signed 'George P.,' and the other 'George Guelph.' I believe them to be gross and rank forgeries. The Court has no difficulty in coming to the conclusion, even assuming that the signatures had that character of genuineness which they have not, that what is asserted in these documents has not the slightest foundation in fact."

With this view the Lord Chief Baron and the Judge-Ordinary entirely concurred, the former adding:

". . . the declarations of Hannah Lightfoot, if there ever was such a person, cannot be received in evidence on the faith of these documents . . . the only issues for the jury are the issues in the cause and this is not an issue in the cause, but an incidental issue. . . . I think that these documents, which the Lord Chief Justice has treated with all the respect which properly belongs to them, are not genuine."

Before the Attorney General had finished the statement of his case, he was interrupted by the foreman of the jury, who said that the jury were unanimously of opinion that there was no necessity to hear any further evidence as they were convinced that the signatures of the documents were not genuine. On this the Lord Chief Justice said:

"You share the opinion which my learned brothers and I have entertained for a long time; that every one of the documents is spurious."

As the Counsel for the Petitioners had "felt it his duty to make some observations to the jury before they delivered their verdict," and had made them, the Lord Chief Justice summed up. Towards the conclusion of his summing-up he said, in speaking of the various conflicting stories put forth by Mrs. Serres:

"In each of the claims which she made at different times, she appealed to documents in her possession by which they were supported. What was the irresistible inference? Why, that documents were from time to time prepared to meet the form which her claims from time to time assumed."

The jury, without hesitation, found that they were not satisfied "that Olive Serres, the mother of

Mrs. Ryves, was the legitimate daughter of Henry Frederick Duke of Cumberland and Olive his wife; and they were not satisfied that Henry Frederick, Duke of Cumberland, was lawfully married to Olive Wilmot on the 4th of March 1767 . . ."

The case of Mrs. Serres is an instance of how a person, otherwise comparatively harmless but afflicted with vanity and egotism, may be led away into evil courses, from which, had she realised their full iniquity, she might have shrunk. The only thing outside the case we have been considering, was that she separated from her husband; which indeed was an affliction rather than a crime. She had been married for thirteen years and had borne two children, but so far as we know no impropriety was ever alleged against her. One of her daughters remained her constant companion till her twenty-second year and through her long life held her and her memory in filial devotion and respect. The forethought, labour and invention which she devoted to the fraud, if properly and honestly used, might have won for her a noteworthy place in the history of her time. But as it was, she frittered away in criminal work her good opportunities and great talents, and ended her life within the rules of the King's Bench.

PARACELSUS

I FEEL that I ought to begin this record with an apology to the *manes* of a great and fearless scholar, as earnest as he was honest, as open-minded as he was great-hearted. I do so because I wish to do what an unimportant man can after the lapse of centuries, to help a younger generation to understand what such a man as I write of can do and did under circumstances not possible in times of greater enlightenment. The lesson which the story can tell to thinking youth cannot be told in vain. The greatest asset which worth has in this world is the irony of time. Contemporaneous opinion, though often correct, is generally on the meagre side of appreciation—practically always so with regard to anything new. Such must in any case be encountered in matters of the sixteenth century which being on the further side of an age of discovery and reform had hardened almost to the stage of ossification the beliefs and methods of the outgoing order of things. Prejudice—especially when it is based on science and religion—dies hard: the very spirit whence originates a stage of progress or reform, makes its inherited follower tenacious of *its* traditions however short they may be. This is why any who, in this later and more open minded age, may investigate the intellectual discoveries of the past, owe a special debt in the way of justice to the memories of those to whom such fresh light is due. The name and story of the individual known as Paracelsus—scholar, scientist, open minded thinker and teacher, earnest investigator and searcher for elemental truths—is a case in point. Anyone who contents himself with accepting the judgment of four centuries passed upon the great Swiss thinker, who had rendered famous in history his place of birth, his canton and his nation, would inevitably come to the conclusion that he was merely a charlatan a little more clever than others of his kind; an acceptor of all manner of eccentric beliefs (including the efficacy of spirits and demons in pathological cases), a drunkard, a wastrel, an evil liver, a practiser of necromancy, an astrologer, a magician, an atheist, an alchemist—indeed an "ist" of all defamatory kinds within the terminology of the sixteenth century and of all disputatious churchmen and scientists who have not agreed with his theories and conclusions ever since.

Let us begin with the facts of his life. His name was Theophrastus Bombast von Hohenheim, and he was the son of a doctor living in Einsiedeln in the canton of Schwyz, named Wilhelm Bombast von Hohenheim, natural son of a Grand Master of the Teutonic Order. He was born in 1490.

It was not uncommon for a man of that age who was striving to make a name for himself, to assume some *nom de plume* or *de guerre;* and with such a family record as his own, it was no wonder that on the threshold of his life the young Theophrastus did so. In the light of his later achievements, we can well imagine that he had some definite purpose in mind, or at least some guiding principle of suggestiveness, in choosing such a compound word from the Greek as Paracelsus (which is derived from "para," meaning before, in the sense of superior to, and Celsus, the name of an Epicurean philosopher of the second century.) Celsus appears to have had views of great enlightenment according to the thought of his own time. Unhappily only fragments of his work remain, but as he was a follower of Epicurus after an interval of between four and five centuries, it is possible to get some idea of his main propositions. Like Epicurus he stood for nature. He did not believe in fatalism, but he did in a supreme power. He was a Platonist and held that there was no truth which was against nature. It is easy to see from his life and work that Theophrastus Bombast von Hohenheim shared his views. His intellectual attitude was that of a true scientist—denying nothing *prima facie* but investigating all.

"There lives more faith in honest doubt,
Believe me, than in half the creeds."

His father moved in 1502 to Villach in Carinthia, where he practised medicine till his death in 1534. Theophrastus was a precocious boy; after youthful study with his father, he entered the University of Basel when he was about sixteen, after which he prosecuted chemical researches under the learned Trithemius Bishop of Sponheim who had written on the subject of the Great elixir —the common subject of the scientists of that day, —and at Wurzburg. From thence he proceeded to the great mines in the Tyrol, then belonging to the Fugger family. Here he studied geology and its kindred branches of learning—especially those dealing with effects and so far as possible with causes—metallurgy, mineral waters, and the diseases of and accidents to mines and miners. The theory of knowledge which he deduced from these studies was that we must learn nature from nature.

In 1527, he returned to Basel, where he was appointed town physician. It was a characteristic of his independence and of his mind, method and design, that he lectured in the language of the place, German, foregoing the Latin tongue, usual up to that time for such teaching. He did not shrink from a bold criticism of the medical ideas and methods then current. The effect of this independence and teaching was that for a couple of years his reputation and his practice increased wonderfully. But the time thus passed allowed his enemies not only to see the danger for them that lay ahead, but to take such action as they could to obviate it. Reactionary forces are generally—if not always—self-protective, without regard to the right or wrong of the matter, and Paracelsus began to find that the self-interest and ignorance of the many were too strong for him, and that their unscrupulous attacks began to injure his work seriously. He was called conjurer, necromancer, and many such terms of obloquy. Then what we may call his "professional" enemies felt themselves strong enough to join in the attack. As he had kept a careful eye on the purity of medicines in use, the apothecaries, who, in those days worked in a smaller field than now, and who found their commerce more productive through guile than excellence, became almost declared opponents. Eventually he had to leave Basel. He went to Esslingen, from which however he had to retire at no distant period from sheer want.

Then began a period of wandering which really lasted for the last dozen years of his life. This time was mainly one of learning in many ways of many things. The ground he covered must have been immense, for he visited Colmar, Nurnberg, Appengall, Zurich, Augsburg, Middelheim, and travelled in Prussia, Austria, Hungary, Egypt, Turkey, Russia, Tartary, Italy, the Low Countries and Denmark. In Germany and Hungary he had a bad time, being driven to supply even the bare necessaries of life by odd—any—means, even to availing himself of the credulity of others—casting nativities, telling fortunes, prescribing remedies for animals of the farm such as cows and pigs, and recovering stolen property; such a life indeed as was the lot of a mediæval "tramp." On the other hand, as a contra he did worthy work as a military surgeon in Italy, the Low Countries and Denmark. When he got tired of his wandering life, he settled down in Salsburg, in 1541, under the care and protection of the Archbishop Ernst. But he did not long survive the prospect of rest; he died later in the same year. The cause of his death is not known with any certainty, but we can guess that he had clamorous enemies as well as strong upholding from the conflicting causes given. Some said that he died from the effects of a protracted debauch, others that he was murdered by physicians and apothecaries, or their agents, who had thrown him over a cliff. In proof of this story it was said that the surgeons had found a flaw or fracture in his skull which must have been produced during life.

He was buried in the churchyard of Saint Sebastian; but two centuries later, 1752, his bones were moved to the porch of the church, and a monument erected over them.

His first book was printed in Augsburg in 1526. His real monument was the collection of his complete writings so far as was possible, the long work of Johann Huser made in 1589–91. This great work was published in German, from printed copy supplemented by such manuscript as could be discovered. Then and ever since there has been a perpetual rain of statements against him and his beliefs. Most of them are too silly for words; but it is a little disconcerting to find one writer of some distinction repeating so late as 1856 all the malignant twaddle of three centuries, saying amongst other things that he believed in the transmutation of metals and the possibility of an *elixir vitæ,* that he boasted of having spirits at his command, one of which he kept imprisoned in the hilt of his sword and another in a jewel; that he could make any one live forever; that he was proud to be called a magician; and had boasted of having a regular correspondence with Galen in Hell. We read in sensational journals and magazines of to-day about certain living persons having—or saying that they have—communion in the shape of "interviews" with the dead; but this is too busy an age for unnecessary contradictions and so such assertions are allowed to pass. The same indifference may now and again have been exhibited in the case of men like Paracelsus.

Some things said of him may be accepted as being partially true, for his was an age of mysticism, occultism, astrology, and all manner of strange and weird beliefs. For instance it is alleged that he held that life is an emanation from the stars; that the sun governed the heart, the moon the brain,

Jupiter the liver, Saturn the gall, Mercury the lungs, Mars the bile, Venus the loins; that in each stomach is a demon, that the belly is the grand laboratory where all the ingredients are apportioned and mixed; and that gold could cure ossification of the heart.

Is it any wonder that when in this age after centuries of progress such absurd things are current Paracelsus is shewn in contemporary and later portraits with a jewel in his hand transcribed Azoth—the name given to his familiar dæmon.

Those who repeat *ad nauseam* the absurd stories of his alchemy generally omit to mention his genuine discoveries and to tell of the wide scope of his teaching. That he used mercury and opium for healing purposes at a time when they were condemned; that he did all he could to stop the practice of administering the vile electuaries of the mediæval pharmacopœia; that he was one of the first to use laudanum; that he perpetually held—to his own detriment—that medical science should not be secret; that he blamed strongly the fashion of his time of accounting for natural phenomena by the intervention of spirits or occult forces; that he deprecated astrology; that he insisted on the proper investigation of the properties of drugs and that they should be used more simply and in smaller doses. To these benefits and reforms his enemies answered that he had made a pact with the devil. For reward of his labours, his genius, his fearless struggle for human good he had—with the exception of a few spells of prosperity—only penury, want, malicious ill-fame and ceaseless attacks by the professors of religion and science. He was an original investigator of open mind, of great ability and application, and absolutely fearless. He was centuries ahead of his time. We can all feel grateful to that French writer who said:

> "Tels sont les services eminents que Paracelse a rendu à l'humanité souffrante, pour laquelle il montra toujours le dévouement le plus désintéressé; s'il en fut mal recompensé pendant sa vie que sa mémoire au moins soit honorée."

CAGLIOSTRO

THE individual known to history as Comte Cagliostro, or more familiarly as Cagliostro, was of the family name of Balsamo and was received into the Church under the saintly name of Joseph. The familiarity of history is an appanage of greatness in some form. Greatness is in no sense a quality of worth or morality. It simply points to publicity, and if unsuccessful, to infamy. Joseph Balsamo was of poor parentage in the town of Palermo, Sicily, and was born in 1743. In his youth he did not exhibit any talent whatever, such volcanic forces as he had being entirely used in wickedness—base, purposeless, sordid wickedness, from which devolved no benefit to any one—even to the the criminal instigator. In order to achieve greatness, or publicity, in any form, some remarkable quality is necessary; Joseph Balsamo's claim was based not on isolated qualities but on a union of many. In fact he appears to have had every necessary ingredient for this kind of success—except one, courage. In his case however, the lacking ingredient in the preparation of his hell-broth was supplied by luck; though such luck had to be paid for at the devil's usual price—

CAGLIOSTRO

failure at the last. His biographers put his leading characteristics in rather a negative than a positive way—"indolent and unruly"; but as time went on the evil became more marked—even *ferae naturae,* poisonous growths, and miasmatic conditions have to manifest themselves or to cease to prevail. In the interval between young boyhood and coming manhood, Balsamo's nature—such as it was—began to develop, unscrupulousness working on an imaginative basis being always a leading characteristic. The unruly boy shewed powers of becoming an unruly man, fear being the only restraining force; and indolence giving way to wickedness. When he was about fifteen he was sent to a monastery to learn chemistry and pharmacy. The boy who had manifested a tendency to "grow downwards" found the beginning of a kind of success in these studies in which, to the surprise of all, he exhibited a form of aptitude. Chemistry has certain charms to a mind like his, for in its working are many strange surprises and lurid effects not unattended with entrancing fears. These he used before long to his own pleasure in the concern of others. When he was expelled from the religious house he led a dissolute and criminal life in Palermo. Amongst other wickednesses he robbed his uncle and forged his will. Here too, he committed a crime, not devoid of a certain humorous aspect, but which had a reflex action on his own life. Under promise of revealing a hidden treasure, he persuaded a goldworker, one Morano, to give him custody of a quantity of his wares. It was what, in criminal slang is called "a put-up job," and was worked by a gang of young thieves with Balsamo at their head. Having filled the soft head of the foolish goldsmith with ideas to suit his purpose, Joseph brought him on a treasure hunt into a cave where he was shortly surrounded by the gang dressed as fiends, who, in the victim's paralysis of fear, robbed him at their ease of some sixty ounces of gold. Morano, as might have been expected, was not satisfied with the proceedings and vowed vengeance which he tried to effect later. Balsamo's pusillanimity worked hand in hand with Morano's vindictiveness, to the effect that the culprit incontinently absconded from his native town. He conferred the benefit of his presence on Messina where he was naturally attracted to a noted alchemist called Althotas, to whom he became a sort of disciple. Althotas was a man of great learning, according to the measure of that time and his own occupation. He was skilled in Eastern tongues and an adept occultist. It was said that he had actually visited Mecca and Medina in the disguise of an Oriental prince. Having attached himself to Althotas, Cagliostro went with him to Malta where he persuaded the Grand Master of the Knights to supply them with a laboratory for the manufacture of gold, and also with letters of introduction which he afterwards used with much benefit to himself.

From Malta he went to Rome where he employed himself in forging engravings. Like other criminals, great and small, Comte Alessandro Cagliostro—as he had now become by his own creation of nobility—had a faculty of working hard and intelligently so long as the end he aimed at was to be accomplished by crooked means. Work in the ordinary ways of honesty he loathed and shunned; but work as a help to his nefarious schemes seemed to be a joy to him. Then he set himself up as a wonder-worker, improving as he went on all the customs and tricks of that calling. He sold an elixir which he said had all the potency usually attributed to such compounds but with an added efficacy all its own. He pretended to be able to transmute metals and to make himself invisible; indeed to perform all the wonders of the alchemist, the "cheap jack," and the charlatan. At Rome he became acquainted with and married a very beautiful woman, Lorenza de Feliciani, daughter of a lacemaker, round whom later biographers weave romances. According to contemporary accounts she seems to have been dowered with just such qualities as were useful in such a life as she had entered on. In addition to great and unusual beauty she was graceful, passionate, seductive, clever, plausible, soothing, and attractive in all ways dear and convincing to men. She must have had some winning charm which has lasted beyond her time, for a hundred years afterwards we find so level-headed a writer as Dr. Charles Mackay crediting her, quite unwarrantably with, amongst other good qualities, being a faithful wife. Her life certainly after her marriage was such that faithfulness in any form was one of the last things to expect in her. Her husband was nothing less than a swindler of a protean kind. He had had a great number of aliases before he finally fixed on Comte de Cagliostro as a *nomme de guerre.* He called himself successively Chevalier de Fischio, Marquis de Melina (or Melissa), Marquis de Pellegrini, Comte de Saint-German, Baron de Belmonte; together with such names as Fenix, Anna, Harat. He wrote a work somewhat of the nature of a novel called *Le Grand Cophte*—which he found useful later when he was pushing his scheme of a sort of new Freemasonry. After his marriage he visited several countries, Egypt, Arabia, Persia, Poland, Russia, Greece, Germany; as well as such towns as Naples, Palermo, Rhodes, Strasbourg, Paris, London, Lisbon, Vienna, Venice, Madrid, Brussels—in fact any place where many fools were crowded into a small space. In many of these he found use for the introductory letters of the Grand Master of the Knights of Malta, as well as those of other dupes from whom it was his habit to secure such letters before the inevitable crash came. Wherever he travelled he was accustomed to learn all he could of the manners, customs and facts of each place he was in, thus accumulating a vast stock of a certain form of knowledge which he found most useful in his chosen occupation—deceit. With regard to the last he utilised every form of human credulity which came under his notice. The latter half of the eighteenth century was the very chosen time of strange beliefs. Occultism became a fashion, especially amongst the richer classes, with the result that every form of swindle came to the fore. At this time Cagliostro, then nearing his fortieth year, began to have a widespread reputation for marvellous cures. As mysticism in all sorts of forms had a vogue, he used all the tricks of the cult, gathering them from various countries, especially France and Germany, where the fashion was pronounced. For this trickery he used all his knowledge of the East and all the picturesque aids to credulity which he had picked up during his years of wandering; and for his "patter," such medical terminology as he had learned—he either became a doctor or invented a title for himself. This he interlarded with scraps of various forms of fraudulent occultism and all sorts of suggestive images of eastern quasi-religious profligacy. He took much of the imagery which he used in his rituals of fraud from records of ancient Egypt. This was a pretty safe ground for his purpose, for in his time the Egypt of the past was a sealed book. It was only in 1799 that the Rosetta stone was discovered, and more than ten years from then before Dr. Young was able to translate its three inscriptions—Hieroglyphic Demotic and Greek—whence Hieroglyphic knowledge had its source. *Omne ignotum pro magnifico* might well serve as a motto for all occultism, true or false. Cagliostro, whose business it was to deceive and mislead, understood this and took care that in his cabalistic forms Egyptian signs were largely mixed with the pentagon, the signs of the Zodiac, and other mysterious symbols in common use. His object was primarily to catch the eye and so arrest the intelligence of any whom he wished to impress. For this purpose he went about gorgeously dressed and with impressive appointments. In Germany for instance he always drove in a carriage with four horses with courier and equerries in striking liveries. Happily there is extant a pen picture of him by Comte de Beugnot who met him in Paris at the house of the Comtesse de la Motte:

> "of medium height and fairly fat, of olive colour, with short neck and round face, big protruberant eyes, a snub nose with open nostrils."

This gives of him anything but an attractive picture; but yet M. de Beugnot says: "he made an impression on women whenever he came into a room." Perhaps his clothing helped, for it was not of a commonplace kind. De Beugnot who was manifestly a careful and intelligent observer again comes to our aid with his pen:

"He wore a coiffure new in France; his hair parted in several little cadenottes (queues or tresses) uniting at the back of the head in the form known as a 'catogan' (hair clubbed or bunched). A dress, French fashion, of iron grey, laced with gold, scarlet waistcoat broidered with bold *point de spain,* red breeches, a basket-hilted sword and a hat with white plumes!"

Aided by these adjuncts he was a great success in Paris whither he returned in 1785. As an impostor he knew his business and played "the game" well. When he was at work he brought to bear the influence of all his "properties," amongst them a tablecloth embroidered with cabalistic signs in scarlet and the symbols of the Rosy Cross of high degree; the same mysterious emblems marked the globe without which no wizard's atelier is complete.

Here too were various little Egyptian figures—"ushabtui" he would doubtless have called them had the word been in use in his day. From these he kept his dupes at a distance, guarding carefully against any discovery. He evidently did not fear to hurt the religious susceptibilities of any of his votaries, for not only were the crucifix and other emblems of the kind placed amongst the curios of his ritual, but he made his invocation in the form of a religious ceremony, going down on his knees and in all ways cultivating the emotions of those round him. He was aided by a young woman whom he described as pure as an angel and of great sensibility. The said young person kept her blue eyes fixed on a globe full of water. Then he proceeded to expound the Great Secret which he told his hearers had been the same since the beginning of things and whose mystery had been guarded by Templars of the Rosy Cross, by Magicians, by Egyptians and the like. He had claimed, as the Comte Saint-German said, that he had already existed for many centuries; that he was a contemporary of Christ; and that he had predicted His crucifixion by the Jews. As statements of this kind were made mainly for the purpose of selling the elixir which he peddled, it may easily be imagined that he did not shrink from lying or blasphemy when such seemed to suit his purpose. Daring and recklessness in his statements seemed to further his business success, so prophecy—or rather boastings of prophecy *after the event*—became part of the great fraud. Amongst other things he said that he had predicted the taking of the Bastille. Such things shed a little light on the methods of such impostors, and help to lay bare the roots or principles through which they flourish.

After his Parisian success he made a prolonged tour in France. In la Vendée he boasted of some fresh miracle—of his own doing—on each day; and at Lyons the boasting was repeated. Of course he occasionally had bad times, for now and again even the demons on whose acquaintance and help he prided himself did not work. In London after 1772, things had become so bad with him that he had to work as a house painter under his own name. Whatever may have been his skill in his art this was probably about the only honest work he ever did. He did not stick to it for long however, for four years afterwards he lost three thousand pounds by frauds of others by whom he was introduced to fictitious lords and ladies. Here too he underwent a term of imprisonment for debt.

Naturally such an impostor found in Freemasonry, which is a secret cult, a way of furthering his ends. With the aid of his wife, who all through their life together seems to have worked with him, he founded a new branch of freemasonry in which a good many rules of that wonderful organisation were set at defiance. As the purpose of the new cult was to defraud, its net was enlarged by taking women into the body. The name used for it was the *Grand Egyptian Lodge*—he being himself the head of it under the title of the *Cophte* and his wife the *Grand Priestess.* In the ritual were some appalling ceremonies, and as these made eventually for profitable publicity, the scheme was a great success—and the elixir sold well. This elixir was the backbone of his revenue; and indeed it would have been well worthy of success if it had been all that he claimed for it. Dispensers of elixirs are not usually backward in proclaiming the virtues of their wares; but in his various settings forth Cagliostro went further than others. He claimed not only to restore youth and health and to make them perpetual, but to restore lost innocence and effect a whole moral regeneration. No wonder that he achieved success and that money rolled in! And no wonder that women, especially of the upper classes, followed him like a flock of sheep! No wonder that a class rich, idle, pleasure-loving, and fond of tasting and testing new sensations, found thrilling moments in the great impostor's mélange of mystery, religion, fear, and hope; of spirit-rapping and a sort of "black mass" in which Christianity and Paganism mingled freely, and where life and death, good and evil, whirled together in a maddening dance.

It was not, however, through his alleged sorcery that Cagliostro crept into a place in history; but by the association of his name with a sordid crime which involved the names of some of the great ones of the earth. The story of the Queen's Necklace, though he was acquitted at the trial which concluded it, will be remembered when the vapourings of the unscrupulous quack who had escaped a thousand penalties justly earned, have been long forgotten. Such is the irony of history! The story of the necklace involved Marie Antoinette, Cardinal Prince de Rohan, Comte de la Motte—an officer of the private guard of "Monsieur" (the Comte d'Artois), his wife Jeanne de Valois, descended from Henry II through Saint-Remy, his natural son and Nicole de Savigny. Louis XV had ordered from MM. Boemer et Bassange, jewellers to the Court of France, a beautiful necklace of extraordinary value for his mistress Madame du Barry, but died before it was completed. The du Barry was exiled by his successor, so the necklace remained on the hands of its makers. It was, however, of so great intrinsic value that they could not easily find a purchaser. They offered it to Marie Antoinette for one million eight hundred thousand livres; but the price was too high even for a queen, and the necklace remained on hand. So Boemer showed it to Madame de la Motte and offered to give a commission on the sale to whoever should find a buyer. She induced her husband, Comte de la Motte, to join with her in a plot to accomplish the sale. De la Motte was a friend of Cagliostro, and he too was brought in as he had influence with the Cardinal Prince de Rohan whom they looked on as a likely person to be of service. He had his own ambitions to acquire influence over the queen and use her for political purposes as Mazarin had used Anne of Austria. De Rohan was then a man of fifty—not considered much of an age in these days, but the Cardinal's life had not made for comparative longevity. He was in fact something of that class of fool which has no peer in folly—an old fool; and Jeanne de la Motte fooled him to the top of his bent. She pretended to him that Marie Antoinette was especially friendly to her, and shewed him letters from the queen to herself all of which had been forged for the purpose. As at this time

Madame de la Motte had borrowed or otherwise obtained from the Cardinal a hundred and twenty thousand livres, she felt assured he could be used for the contemplated fraud. She probably had not ever even spoken to the queen but she was not scrupulous in such a small matter as one more untruth. She finally persuaded him that Marie Antoinette wished to purchase the necklace through his agency, he acting for her and buying it in her name. To aid in the scheme she got her pet forger, Retaux de Vilette, to prepare a receipt signed "Marie Antoinette de France." The Cardinal fell into the trap and obtained the jewel, giving to Boemer four bills due successively at intervals of six months. At Versailles de Rohan gave the casket containing the necklace to Madame de la Motte, who in his presence handed it to a valet of the royal household for conveyance to the queen. The valet was none other than the forger Retaux de Vilette. Madame de la Motte sent to the Cardinal a letter by the same forger asking him to meet her (the queen) in the shrubbery at Versailles between eleven o'clock and midnight. To complete the deception a girl was procured, one Olivia, who in figure resembled the queen sufficiently to pass for her in the dusk. The meeting between de Rohan and the alleged queen was held at the Baths of Apollo—to the deception and temporary satisfaction of the ambitious churchman. When the first instalment for the purchase of the necklace was due,

Boemer tried to find out if the queen really had possession of the necklace—which had in the meanwhile been brought to London, it was said, by Comte de la Motte. As Boemer could not manage to get an audience with the queen he came to the conclusion that he had been robbed, and made the matter public. This was reported to M. de Breteuil, Master of the King's household, and an enemy of de Rohan. De Breteuil saw the queen secretly and they agreed to act in concert in the matter. Louis XVI asked for details of the purchase from Boemer, who told the truth so far as he knew it, producing as a proof the alleged receipt of the queen. Louis pointed out to him that he should have known that the queen did not sign after the manner of the document. He then asked de Rohan, who was Grand Almoner of France, for his written justification. This being supplied, he had him arrested and sent to the Bastille. Madame de la Motte accused Cagliostro of the crime, alleging that he had persuaded de Rohan to buy the necklace. She was also arrested as were Retaux de Vilette, and, later on at Brussels, Olivia, who threw some light on the fraud. The King brought the whole matter before Parliament, which ordered a prosecution. As the result of the trial which followed, Comte de la Motte and Retaux de Vilette were banished for life; Jeanne de la Motte was condemned to make *amende honourable,* to be whipped and branded with V on both shoulders, and to be imprisoned for life. Olivia and Cagliostro were acquitted. The Cardinal was cleared of all charges. Nothing seems to have been done for the poor jewellers, who, after all, had received more substantial injury than any of the others, having lost nearly two million livres.

After the affair of the Necklace, Cagliostro spent a time in the Bastille and when free, after some months, he and his wife travelled again in Europe. In 1789 he was arrested at Rome by order of the Inquisition and condemned to death as a Freemason. The punishment was later commuted to perpetual imprisonment. He ended his days in the Château de Saint-Leon near Rome. His wife was condemned to perpetual seclusion and died in the Convent of Sainte-Appolive.

MESMER

ALTHOUGH Frederic-Antoine Mesmer made an astonishing discovery which, having been tested and employed in therapeutics for a century, is accepted as a contribution to science, he is included in the list of impostors because, however sound his theory was, he used it in the manner or surrounded with the atmosphere of imposture. Indeed the implement which he used in his practice, and which made him famous in fashionable and idle society, was set forth as having magic properties. He belonged to the same period as Cagliostro, having been born but nine years before him, in 1734, in Itzmang, Suabia; but the impostor pure and simple easily picked up the difference by beginning his life-work earlier and following it quicker with regard to results. Mesmer was not in any sense a precocious person. He was thirty-two years of age when he took his degree of Doctor of Medicine at Vienna in 1765. However he had already chosen his subject, animal magnetism as allied with medical therapeutics. His early script under the title *De planetarum influxi* is looked on as a legal reminiscence of judicial astronomy. He left Vienna because, he said, of a cabal against him, and travelled in Europe, particularly in Switzerland, before he went to Paris to seek his fortune. This was in 1778, when he was some forty-four years of age; his reputation, which had been growing all the time, preceded him. He was then a man of fine appearance, tall and important-looking and conveying a sense of calm power. He produced much sensation and was at once credited—not without his own will or intention—with magic power. He posed as a benefactor of humanity; a position which was at once conceded to him, partly owing to the fact that an extraordinary atmosphere of calm seemed to surround him, which with his natural air of assurance founded on self-belief, was able to convey to his patients a sense of hope which was of course very helpful in cases of nervous failure and depression. He settled in the Hotel Bouret near the Place Vendôme and so in the heart of Paris; and at once undertook the treatment of patients hitherto deemed incurable. Fashion took up the new medical "craze" or "sensation," and he at once became the vogue. It was at this time of his life that Mesmer came to the parting of the ways between earnest science and charlatanism. So far as we know he still remained earnest in his scientific belief—as indeed he was till the end of his days. Inasmuch as fashion requires some concrete expression of its fancies, Mesmer soon used the picturesque side of his brain for the service of fashionable success. So he invented an appliance which soon became the talk of the town. This was the famous *baquet magique* or magic tub, a sort of covered bath, round which his patients were arranged in tiers. To the bath were attached a number of tubes, each of which was held by a patient, who could touch with the end of it any part of his or her body at will. After a while the patients began to get excited, and many of them went into convulsions. Amongst them walked Mesmer, clad in an imposing dress suggestive of mystery and carrying a long wand of alleged magic power; often calming those who had already reached the stage of being actually convulsed. His usual method of producing something of the same effect at private séances, was by holding the hand of the patient, touching the forehead and making "passes" with the open hand with fingers spread out, and by crossing and uncrossing his arms with great rapidity.

A well-attended séance must have been a curious and not altogether pleasant experience even to a wholesome spectator in full possession of his natural faculties. The whole surroundings of the place together with the previously cultured belief; the dusk and mystery; the "mysterious sympathy of numbers"—as Dean Farrar called it; the spasmodic snapping of the cords of tensity which took away all traces of reserve or reticence from the men and women present; the vague terror of the unknown, that mysterious apprehension which is so potent with the nerves of weak or imaginative people; and, it may be, the slipping of the dogs of conscience—all these combined to wreck the moral and mental stability of those present, most of whom it must be remembered were actually ill, or imagined themselves to be so, which came practically to the same thing. The psychical emotion was all very well in the world of pleasure; but these creatures became physically sick through nervous strain. As described by the historian, they expectorated freely a viscous fluid, and their sickness passed into convulsions more or less violent; the women naturally succumbing more readily and more quickly than the men. This absolute collapse—half epileptic, half hysterical—lasted varying periods according to the influence exercised by the presence of the calm, self-reliant operator. We of a later age, when electric force has been satisfactorily harnessed and when magnetism as a separate power is better understood, may find it hard to understand that the most advanced and daring scientists of the time—to whom Frederic-Antoine Mesmer was at least allied—were satisfied that magnetism and electricity were variants of the same mysterious force or power. It was on this theory that he seems to have worked his main idea to practical effect. The base of his system was animal magnetism, which could be superinduced or aided by mechanical appliances. He did not deceive himself into believing that he had invented the idea but was quite willing to make the utmost use he could of the discoveries and inventions of others. So far as we can gather his intentions from his acts, the main object in his scientific work was to simplify the processes of turning emotion into effect. Magnetism had already been largely studied, and means were being constantly sought for increasing its efficacy. Father Hehl had brought to a point of accepted perfection the manufacture of metal plates used in magnetic development, and these Mesmer used, with the result that a violent controversy took place between them. So far as we can follow after the lapse of time, Mesmer was consistent in his theories and their application. He held that the principle was one of planetary influence on the nervous system, and its manifestation was by a process of alternate intension and remission. It is possible that Mesmer—who held that the heavenly bodies floated in a limitless magnetic fluid and that he could make all substances, even such things as bread or dogs magnetic—had in his mind the wisdom of following the same theory in matters of lesser significance, though of more individual import, than those of astronomy and its correlated sciences. If so he was wise in his generation, for later electricians have found that the system of alternating currents especially at high tension, is of vast practical importance. That he was practical in his use of the ideas of others is shown by the fact that he preferred the metallic plates of Father Hehl to his own passes, even though the report of the Royal Commission ruined him—at any rate checked his success, by stating that similar effects to those attending his passes could be produced by other means, and that such passes had no effect unless through the patient's knowledge; in fact that it was all the work of imagination. Mesmer had been asked to appear before the Commission of the Faculty of Medicine appointed in 1784 to investigate and report, but he kept away. It would not have injured any man to have appeared before such a commission if his cause had been a good one. There were two such commissions. The first was of the leading physicians of Paris, and included such men as Benjamin Franklin, Lavoisier, the great chemist, and Bailly, the historian of astronomy.

It was distinctly to his disadvantage that Mesmer always kept at a distance the whole corps of savants such as the Faculty of Medicine and the Academy of Sciences—for they would no doubt have accepted his views, visionary though they were, if he could have shown any scientific base for them. True medical science has always been suspicious of, and cautious regarding, empiricism. More than once he stood in his own light in this matter—whether through obstinacy or doubt of his own theory does not matter. For instance, in Vienna, when his very existence as a scientist was at stake in the matter of the effects of his treatment of Mademoiselle Paradis, he introduced a humiliating clause in his challenge to the Faculty which caused them to refuse to accept it. Mademoiselle Paradis was blind and subject to convulsions. After treating her by his own method Mesmer said she was cured. An oculist said, after testing, that she was as blind as ever, and her family said that she was still subject to convulsions. But Mesmer persisted that she was cured, that there was a conspiracy against him, and that Mademoiselle Paradis had feigned. He challenged the Faculty of Medicine on the subject of his discovery. Twenty-four patients were to be selected by the Faculty; of these twelve were to be treated by Mesmerism and the other half by the means ordinarily in use. The condition he imposed was that the witnesses were *not* to be of the Faculty.

Again, when in answer to a request on his part that the French Government for the good of the community should subsidise him, a proposal was made to him, he did not receive it favourably. The request he made to Marie Antoinette was that he should have an estate and château and a handsome income, so that he might go on experimenting; he put the broad figures at four hundred or five hundred thousand francs. The Government suggestion was that he should have a pension of twenty thousand francs and the Cross of Saint Michael (Knighthood) if he would communicate for public use, to a board of physicians nominated by the King, such discoveries as he might make. After his refusal of the Government proposition Mesmer went to Spa, taking with him a number of his patients, and there opened a magnetic establishment where he renewed his Paris success. He asked Parliament to hold an impartial examination into the theory and working of Animal Magnetism. Foiled in his scheme of state purchase on his own terms, he sold his secret to a group of societies, the members of which were to pay him a subscription of a hundred louis *per capita.* By this means he realised some 340,000 livres—representing to-day over a million. The associated body was composed of twenty-four societies called "societés de l'harmonie"—a sort of Freemasonry, under a Grand Master and Chiefs of the Order. A member had to be at the time of admission twenty-five years of age, of honest state and good name, not to smoke tobacco, and to pay an annual subscription of at least sixty francs. There were three grades in the Order: Initiated Associates, Corresponding Associates and Uninitiated. Amongst those belonging to the Society were such men as Lafayette, d'Espremisnil, and Berthollet the great chemist. Berthollet had, however, peculiar privileges, amongst which was the right of criticism. On one occasion he had a "row" with Mesmer about his charlatanism.

At length the French public, wearied with his trickeries and angry with his cupidity, openly expressed their dissatisfaction. Whereupon he left France, taking with him a fortune of three hundred and forty thousand francs. He went to England and thence to Germany. Finally he settled down in Mersbourg in his native country, Suabia, where he died in 1815, at the age of eighty-one.

THE WANDERING JEW

THE legend of the Wandering Jew has its roots in a belief in the possibility of human longevity beyond what is natural and normal. It is connected with the story of the Crucifixion and the mysteries that preceded and followed it. Our account may find its starting point in a book of extraordinary interest which made a sensation in the seventeenth century and is still delightful reading. The passage which should arrest our attention is as follows:

"The story of the Wandering Jew is very strange and will hardly obtain belief; yet there is a small account thereof set down by *Matthew Paris* from the report of an Armenian Bishop; who came into this Kingdom about four hundred years ago, and had often entertained this wanderer at his Table. That he was then alive, was first called *Cartaphilus,* was keeper of the Judgment Hall, whence thrusting out our Saviour with expostulation of his stay, was condemned to stay until His return; was after baptized by *Ananias,* and by the name of Joseph; was thirty years old in the dayes of our Saviour, remembered the Saints that arised with Him, the making of the Apostles' Creed, and their several peregrinations. Surely were this true, he might be an happy arbitrator in many Christian controversies; but must impardonably condemn the obstinacy of the Jews, who can contemn the Rhetorick of such miracles, and blindly behold so living and lasting conversions."

The above is taken from the work entitled "Pseudoxia Epidemica" or Enquiries into very many Received Tenets and Commonly Presumed Truths by Sir Thomas Brown, Knight M.D. This was first published in 1640, so that the "about four hundred years ago" mentioned would bring the report of the Armenian Bishop to the first half of the thirteenth century.

Thus unless there be something of an authoritative character to upset the theory, Matthew Paris must be taken as the first European narrator of the story. As a matter of fact the legend began just about the time thus arrived at. The great work in Latin, *"Historia Major,"* was begun by Roger of Wendover and completed in 1259 by the monk Matthew Paris. It was not however published—in our ordinary sense of the word—until the beginning of the year 1571 when Archbishop Parker took it in hand. In the meantime the art of printing had been established and the new world of thought and the reproduction of its fruit, had been developed for common use. The *Historia Major* was again printed in Zurich in 1589 and 1606. The next English edition was in 1640. This was reprinted in Paris in 1644. The English edition of forty years later, 1684, was a really fine specimen of typographic art. The authorship and date of its printing are given: Matthaei Paris, Monachi Albanensis

Angli London MDCLXXXIV. The script is in ecclesiastical Latin and to any modern reader is of a fresh and almost child-like sincerity which at once disarms doubt or hostile criticism. Indeed it affords a good example of the mechanism of myth, showing how the littleness of human nature —vanity with its desire to shine and credulity in its primitive form, are not subject to the controlling influences of either sacredness of subject or the rulings of common sense. It lends another meaning to the quotation of Feste, the jester: *Cucullus non facit Monachum.* The artless narrative recorded in the *Historia Major* makes the whole inception of the myth transparent. In the monastery of St. Albans a conversation is held by the monks on one side and the Armenian Archbishop —name not given, on the other. The interpreter in French is one Henri Spigurnel a native of Antioch, servant of the bishop. We can gather even how Sir Thomas Brown M. D., doctor of Norwich and most open-minded of scientists, lent himself, unconsciously, to the propagation of error. Brown reading, or hearing read, the work of Matthew Paris took it for granted that the record was correct and complete; and in his own book summarises or generalises the statements made. For instance he says that the Armenian bishop had "often entertained this wanderer at his table" &c. Now it was his servant who told the monks that the wandering Jew whom he had seen and heard speaking many times dined at the table of his lord the Archbishop. This at once minimises the value of the statement, for it does away at once with the respect due to the bishop's high office and presumed character, and with the sense of intellectual acumen and accuracy which might be expected to emanate from one of his scholarship and quality. Thus we get the story not from an accredited Bishop on a foreign mission—rare at the period and entrusted only to men of note—but from the gossip of an Armenian lacquey or valet, trying to show his own importance to a credulous serving brother of the monastery. And so, after all, coming from this source it is to be accepted with exceeding care—not to say doubt, even when seconded by the learned monastic scribe Matthew. So, also, for instance is his statement regarding the manner in which the wanderer's life is miraculously prolonged. It is to this effect. Each hundredth year Joseph falls into a faint so that he lies for a time unconscious. When he recovers he finds that his age is restored to that which it was when the Lord suffered. Joseph, it must be borne in mind, is the Wandering Jew, once Cartaphilus, who had kept Pilate's judgment-hall. Then Matthew himself takes up the story and gives what professes to be the *ipsissima verba* of the servant as to the conversation between Christ and Cartaphilus which culminated in the terrible doom pronounced on the janitor who, from the showing, did not seem a whit worse than any of the crowd present on that momentous day in Jerusalem. When Jesus, wearied already with carrying the great cross, leaned for a moment against the wall of the house of Cartaphilus just opposite the Judgment-hall the official said:

> "'Vade Jesu citius, vade, quid moraris?' et Jesus severo vultu et oculo respiciens eum, dixit: 'Ego vado. Expectabis donec veniam.'"

Now this is the whole and sole foundation of the individual Wandering Jew. I say "individual" because there were before long other variants, and many old beliefs and fables were appropriated and used to back up the marvellous story, invented by the Armenian servant and recorded by the learned monk, Matthew. Amongst these beliefs were those which taught that John the Baptist never died; that the aloe blooms only once in a hundred years; and that the phœnix renews itself in fire. It is the tendency of legendary beliefs to group or neucleate themselves as though there were a conscious and intentional effort at self-protection; and this, together with the natural human tendency to enlarge and elaborate an accepted idea, is responsible for much. The legend started in the thirteenth century, took root and flourished, and in the very beginning of the seventeenth a variant blossomed. In this Joseph, originally Cartaphilus, became Ahasuerus. In the long pause the story, after the manner of all things of earth, had grown, details not being lacking. The world was informed through the Bishop of Schleswig, how in 1547, at Hamburg, a man was seen in the Cathedral who arrested attention—why we are not told. He was about fifty years of age, of reverend manner, and dressed in ragged clothes; he bowed low at the name of Christ. Many of the nobility and gentry who saw him recognised him as one whom they had already seen in various places—England, France, Italy, Hungary, Persia, Spain, Poland, Moscow, Lieffland, Sweden, Denmark, Scotland, &c. Inquiry being made of him, he told the Bishop that he was Ahasuerus the shoe-maker of Jerusalem, who had been present at the Crucifixion and had ever since been always wandering. He was well posted in history, especially regarding the lives and sufferings of the Apostles, and told how, when he had directed Christ to move on, the latter had answered: "I will stand here and rest, but thou shalt move on till the last day." He had been first seen, we are told, at Lubeck.

It is strange that in an age of religious domination many of the legends of Our Saviour seem to have been based on just such intolerant anger at personal slight as might have ruled a short-tempered, vain man. For instance look at one of the Christ legends which was reproduced in poor Ophelia's distracted mind apropos of the owl, "They say, the owl was a baker's daughter." The Gloucestershire legend runs that Christ having asked for bread at baking time the mistress of the bakery took dough from the oven, but her daughter having remonstrated as to the size of the benefaction was turned into an owl. The penalty inflicted on the erring janitor of the Presidium is another instance.

The "Wandering Jew" legend once started, was hard to suppress. The thirteenth, fourteenth, fifteenth and sixteenth centuries were the ages of Jew-baiting in the kingdoms of the West, and naturally the stories took their colour from the prevailing idea.

In 1644, Westphalus learned from various sources that the Wandering Jew healed diseases, and that he had said he was at Rome when it was burned by Nero; that he had seen the return of Saladin after his Eastern Conquests; that he had been in Constantinople when Salimen had built the royal mosque; that he knew Tamerlane the Scythian, and Scander Beg, Prince of Epirus; that he had seen Bajazet carried in a cage by Tamerlane's order; that he remembered the Caliphs of Babylon and of Egypt, the Empire of the Saracens, and the Crusades where he had known Godfrey de Bouillon. Amongst other things he seems to have apologised for not seeing the Sack of Jerusalem, because he was at that time in Rome at the Court of Vespasian.

The Ahasuerus version of the Wandering Jew legend seems to have been the popular one amongst the commonalty in England. As an instance might be quoted the broad-sheet ballad of 1670. It is not without even historical significance as it marks the measure of the time in many ways. It is headed: "The Wandering Jew, or the Shoemaker of Jerusalem who lived when Our Lord and Saviour Jesus Christ was crucified appointed by Him to live until Coming again. Tune, *The Lady's Fall* &c. Licens'd and Enter'd according to order." The imprint runs: "Printed by and for W. O. and sold by the Booksellers of Pye-corner and London-Bridge."

A century and a half later—1828—was published a much more pretentious work on the same theme. This was a novel written by Rev. George Croly. It was called: "Salathiel: a Story of the Past, the Present, the Future." It was published anonymously and had an immediate and lasting success. It was founded on historical lines, the author manifestly benefiting by the hints afforded by the work of that consummate liar (in a historical sense) Westphalus—or his informant. Croly was a strange man with a somewhat abnormal faculty of abstraction. I used to hear of him from my father who was a friend of his about a hundred years ago. Being of gentle nature he did not wish to cause any pain or concern to his family or dependents; but at the same time he, as a writer, had to guard himself against interruption and consequent digression of his thoughts during the times he set apart for imaginative work. So he devised a scheme which might often be put in practice with advantage by others similarly employed. When settling down to a spell of such work—which as every creative writer knows involves periods of mental abstraction though of bodily restlessness—he would stick an adhesive wafer on his forehead. The rule of the house was that when he might be adorned in this wise no one was to speak to him, or even notice him, except under special necessity.

The great vogue of *Salathiel* lasted some ten or more years, when the torch of the Wandering Jew was lighted by Eugene Sue the French novelist who had just completed in the *Débats* his story "Les Mystères de Paris." As its successor he chose the theme adopted by Croly, and the new novel *Le Juif-Errant* ran with overwhelming success in the *Constitutionnel.*

Sue was what in modern slang is called "up to date." He knew every trick and dodge of the world of advertisement, and in conjunction with his editor, Dr. Veron, he used them all. But he had good wares to exploit. His novels are really excellent, though the changes in social life and in religious, political and artistic matters, which took place between 1844 and 1910, make some things in them seem out of date. His great imagination, and his firm and rapid grasp of salient facts susceptible of being advantageously used in narrative, pointed out to him a fresh road. It was not sufficient to the hour and place that Cartaphilus—or Joseph—or Ahasuerus, or Salathiel or whatever he might be called—should purge his sin by his personal sufferings alone. In the legend, up to then accepted, he had long ago repented; so to increase the poignancy of his sufferings, Sue took from the experience of his own time a means of embittering the very inmost soul of such an one. He must be made to feel that his existence is a curse not only to himself but to all the world. To this end he attached to the Wanderer the obligation of carrying a fell disease. The quick brain of the great *feuilletonist* seized the dramatic moment for utilising the occasion. A dozen years before, the frightful spread of the cholera, which had once again wrought havoc, woke the whole world to new terror. Some one of uneasy mind who found diversion in obscure comparisons, noted from the records of the disease that its moving showed the same progress in a given direction as a man's walking. A hint was sufficient for the public who eagerly seized the idea that the Wandering Jew had, from the first recorded appearance of the cholera, been the fated carrier of that dreaded pestilence. The idea seemed to be a dramatic inspiration and had prehensile grasp. Great as had been the success of the *Mysteries of Paris,* that of *The Wandering Jew* surpassed it, and for half a century the new novel kept vividly before its readers the old tradition, and so brought it down to the present.

We may now begin to ask ourselves who and where in this great deception was the impostor. Who was the guilty one? And at first glance we are inclined to say "There is none! Whatever the error, mistake, deception, or false conclusion, there has been no direct guilt." This is to presuppose that guilt is of conscious premeditation; and neither intention of evil nor consciousness of guilt is apparent. In legal phrase the *mens rea* is lacking.

It is a purely metaphysical speculation whether guilt is a necessary element of imposition. One is an intellectual experience, the other is an ethical problem; and if we are content to deal with responsibility for another's misdoing, the question of the degree of blameworthiness is sufficient. Let us try a process of exclusions. The complete list of those who had a part in the misunderstanding regarding the myth of the Wandering Jew, leaving out the ostensible fictionists, were:

The Abbot of St. Albans, the Archbishop of Armenia, the interpreter, the Archbishop's servant, the monks or laybrothers who singly or in general conversed with any of the above; and finally Matthew Paris who recorded the story in its various phases. Of these we must except from all blame both the Abbot of St. Albans and the Archbishop of Armenia, both of whom were good grave men of high character and to each of whom had been entrusted matters of the highest concern. The interpreter seems to have only fulfilled his office with exactitude; if in any way or part he used his opportunity to impose on the ignorance of the host or the guest there is no record, no suggestion of it. Matthew Paris was a man of such keenness of mind, of such observation and of such critical insight, that even to-day, after a lapse of over five hundred years, and the withstanding of all the tests of a new intellectual world which included such inventions as printing and photography, he is looked upon as one of the ablest of chroniclers. Moreover he put no new matter nor comments of his own into the wonderful and startling narratives which he was called on to record. He even hints at or infers his own doubt as to the statements made. The monks, servants and others mentioned generally, were merely credulous, simple people of the time, with reverence for any story regarding the *Via Dolorosa,* and respect or awe for those in high places.

There remains but the servant of the foreign Archbishop. It is to him that we must look for any outrage on our normal beliefs. He was manifestly a person of individually small importance—even Matthew Paris whose trained work it was to record with exactness, and whose duty it therefore was to sustain or buttress main facts, did not think it necessary or worth while to mention his name. He had in himself none of the dignity, honour, weight, learning or position of the noble of the Church who was the Abbot's guest. He was after all but a personal servant; probably one of readiness and expediency with a quick imagination and a glib tongue. One who could wriggle through a difficult position, defend himself with ready acquiescence, gain his ends of securing his master's ease, and find all necessary doors open through the bonhommie of his fellow servitors. Such an one accustomed to the exigencies of foreign travel, must have picked up many quaint conceits, legends and japes, and was doubtless a *persona grata* liked and looked up to by persons of his own class, sanctified to some little extent by the reflected glory of his master's great position. It is more than likely that he had been the recipient of many confidences regarding legend and conjecture concerning sacred matters, and that any such legend as he spoke of would have been imparted under conditions favourable to his own comfort. After the manner of his kind his stories doubtless lost nothing in the telling and gained considerably in the re-telling. Even in the short record of Matthew Paris, there is evidence of this in the way in which, after the striking story of Cartaphilus has been told, he returns to the matter again, adding picturesque and inconclusive details of the manner of the centennial renewal of the wanderer's youth. The simplest analysis here will show the falsity of the story; what the great logician Archbishop Whately always insisted on—"internal evidence"—is dead against the Armenian valet, courier, or servitor.

He gave circumstantial account of the periodic illness, loss of memory, and recovery of youth on the part of Cartaphilus; but there is no hint of how he came to know it, and Cartaphilus could not have told him, nor anybody else. We may, I think, take it for granted that no other mere mortal was present, for, had any other human being been there, all the quacksalvers of a thousand miles around would have moved heaven and earth to get information of what was going on, since in mediæval days there was nearly as much competition in the world of charlatanism as there is to-day in the world of sport. The Armenian was much too handy a man at such a crisis to be found out, so we may give him the benefit of the doubt and at once credit him with invention. It is hard to understand—or even to believe without understanding—that so mighty a legend and one so tenacious of life, arose and grew from such a beginning. And yet it is in accord with the irony of nature that one who has unintentionally and unwittingly achieved a publicity which would dwarf the malign reputation of Herostratus should have his name unrecorded.

JOHN LAW

THE MISSISSIPPI SCHEME AND ITS ANTECEDENTS

THE great "Mississippi Scheme" which wrought havoc on the French in 1720 is the central and turning point in the history of John Law, late of Lauriston, Controller-General of Finance in France. His father, William Law (grand nephew of James Law, Archbishop of Glasgow) was a goldsmith in that city.

As in the seventeenth century the goldsmiths were also the bankers and moneylenders of the community, a successful goldsmith might be looked on as on the highroad to great fortune. To William Law in 1671 was born his first son John, who had considerable natural talent in the way of mathematics—and a nature which was such as to nullify their use. As a youth he showed proficiency in arithmetic and algebra, but as he was also in those early days riotous and dissipated, we may fairly come to the conclusion that he did not use his natural powers to their best advantage. He was already a gambler of a marked kind. Before he was of age he was already in debt and was squandering his patrimony. He sold the estate of Lauriston which his thrifty father had acquired, and gave himself over to a life of so-called pleasure. His mother, who had family ambitions, bought the estate so that it might remain in the family of its new possessors. He removed himself to London where within a couple of years he was sentenced to death for murder—not a vulgar premeditated murder for gain, but the unhappy result of a duel wherein he had killed his opponent, a boon companion, one Austin who had acquired the soubriquet of "Beau" Austin. Through social influence the death penalty was commuted for imprisonment, and the crime only regarded as manslaughter. He had however to deal with the relatives of the dead man who were naturally vindictive. One of them entered an appeal against the commutation of the sentence. Law, with the characteristic prudence of his time and nationality, did not wait for the leisurely settlement of the legal process, but escaped to the continent where he remained for some years sojourning in various places. Being naturally clever and daring he seems to have generally fallen on his feet. Whilst in Holland he became secretary to an important official in the diplomatic world, from which service he drifted into an employment with the Bank of Amsterdam. Here the natural bent of his mind found expression. Banking in some of its forms is gambling, and as he was both banker and gambler—one by inherited tendency and the other by personal disposition—he began to find his vogue, addressing himself seriously

JOHN LAW

to the intricacies and possibilities of the profession of banking. He was back in Scotland in 1701 (a risky venture on his part for his felony had not been "purged") and published a pamphlet, *"Proposals and Reasons for constituting a Council of Trade in Scotland."* This he followed up after some years, with another pamphlet, *"Money and Trade considered, with a proposal for supplying the Nation with Money"*; and in the same year (1709) he propounded to the Scotch Parliament a scheme for a State Bank on the security of land—a venture which on being tried speedily collapsed. This, like other schemes of that period, was based on the issue and use of paper money.

In the meantime, and for five or six years afterwards, he was travelling variously throughout Europe, occupying himself with formulating successive schemes of finance, and in gambling—a process in which he, being both skilled and lucky, amassed a sum of over a hundred thousand pounds. He had varying fortunes, however, and was expelled from several cities. He was not without believers in his powers. Amongst them was the Earl of Stair, then Ambassador to France, who allured by his specious methods of finance, suggested to the Earl of Stanhope that he might be useful in devising a scheme for paying off the British National Debt. After the death of Louis XIV, in 1715, he suggested to the Duke of Orleans, the Regent for the young King (Louis XV), the formation of a State Bank. The Regent favoured the idea, but his advisers were against it; it was, however, agreed that Law might found a bank with power to issue notes and accept deposits. This was done by Letters Patent and the *Banque Générale* came into existence in 1710, and was an immediate success. Its principle was to issue paper money which was to be repayable by coin. Its paper rose to a premium in 1716; in 1717 there was a decree that it was to be accepted in the payment of taxes. This created a new form of cheap money, with the result that there was a great and sudden extension of industry and trade. From this rose the idea of a new enterprise—The Mississippi Company—which was to outvie the success of the East India Company incorporated by Charter in 1600 under the title of "The Governor and Company of the Merchants of London trading to the East Indies," which after periods of doubtful fortune, and having become consolidated with its rival "The General East India Company"—partially in 1702, and completely in 1708, under the somewhat elephantine name of "The United Company of Merchants of England trading to the East Indies"—was now a vast organization of national importance. To the new French Company for exploiting the Mississippi Valley was made over Louisiana (which then included what were afterwards the States of Ohio and Missouri). The Decree of Incorporation was issued in 1717. The

Parliament at Paris presently grew jealous of such a concession having been given to a foreigner; and the next year a rumour went about that Parliament was about to have him arrested, tried, and hanged. The Regent met the parliamentary resistance by making (1718) the *Banque Générale* into the *Banque Royale*—the King guaranteeing the notes. Law was made Director General; but he was unable to prevent the Regent from increasing the issue of paper money, by which means he managed to satisfy dishonestly his own extravagance. It was a fiscal principle of the time that the State accountants did not go behind the King's receipt—the *acquit de comptant* as it was called.

The Western Company was enlarged in 1718 by a grant of a monopoly of tobacco, and of the rights of trading ships and merchandise of the Company of Senegal. In 1719, the *Banque Royale* absorbed the rights of the East India and China Companies, and then assumed the all-embracing title of *Compagnie des Indes.* The next year it took in the African Company; and so through that the whole of the non-European trade of France. In 1719, the management of the Mint was handed over to Law's Company; and he was thus enabled to manipulate the coinage. In the same year he had undertaken to pay off the French National Debt, and so become the sole creditor of the Nation. He already exercised the functions of Receiver General and had revenue-farming abolished in its favour. He now controlled the collection and disposal of the whole of the State taxation. At this stage of his adventure, Law seemed a good fiscal administrator. He repealed or reduced pressing taxes on useful commodities, and reduced the price of necessaries by forty per cent. so that the peasants could increase the value of their holdings and their crops without fear of coming later into the remorseless grip of the tax-farmer under the infamous *metayer* system. Free-trade was in the Provinces practically established. This, so far as it went, was all Law's doing. Turgot, who later got credit for what had been done, only carried out what the Scotch financier had planned.

Law had promised high dividends to the speculators in his scheme, and had so far paid them; so it was no wonder that "The System" raised its head again. In 1719–20, all France seemed to flock to Paris to such a degree and with such unanimity of purpose, that it was difficult to obtain room to go on with the necessary work of the Mississippi Scheme. In such matters, resting on human greed which throws all prudence to the winds, the pressure is always towards the centre; and the narrow street of Quin cam poix became a seething mass, day and night, of speculators in a hurry to buy shares. The time for trying to sell them had not yet arrived.

Naturally such a locality rose in value, and as demand emphasises paucity of space, extraordinary prices ruled. Even a small share in the lucky street, where fortunes could be made in an hour, rose to fabulous value. Houses formerly letting for forty pounds a year now fetched eight hundred pounds per month. And no wonder, when shares of the face value of five hundred livres sold for ten thousand! When there is such an overwhelming desire to buy, then is the opportunity for sellers to realise, and the time for such speculation on the one side, and for such commerce on the other, is naturally short and the need pressing.

At the beginning of 1720 everything seemed to be increasing in a sort of geometric ratio. After a dividend of forty per cent. had been declared, shares of five hundred value rose to eighteen thousand. Greed, and the opportunity for satisfying its craving, turned the heads of ordinarily sensible people. The whole world seemed mad. It appeared right enough that the financial wonder-worker who had created such a state of things should be loaded with additional honours. It was only scriptural that he who had already multiplied his talents should be entrusted with more. There was universal rejoicing when John Law—exiled foreigner and condemned murderer—was appointed, in January, 1720, Controller-General of the whole finances of France. Naturally enough, even the hard head of the canny Scot began to manifest symptoms of giving way in the shape of becoming *exalté*. And naturally enough his enemies—financial, political and racial—did not lose the opportunities afforded them of taking advantage of it. Tongues began to wag, and all sorts of rumours, some of them reconcilable with common sense and easily credible, others outrageous, began to go about. Lord Stair reported that Law had boasted that he would raise France on the ruins of England and Holland, to a greater height than she had ever reached; that he could crush the East India Company and even destroy British trade and credit when he chose. Stair resented this, and he and Law from being close friends became enemies. To appease the incensed and at present all-powerful Law, the powers that were recalled Lord Stair.

On 23 February 1720, the *Compagnie des Indes* and the *Banque Royale* were united, thus linking the ends of the financial chain. "The System" was now complete.

When Aladdin set the Genius, who had hitherto worked so willingly, the final task of hanging a roc's egg in the centre of the newly-created palace, he brought the whole structure tumbling about his ears. So it was with John Law and the egregious Mississippi Scheme. His idea was complete and perfect. But the high sun when it reaches its meridianal splendour begins from that instant its downward course.

The reaction was not long in manifesting itself. Usually in such matters there is a pause before the great driving-wheels reverse their motion, and the backward motion, beginning slowly, gathers way as it progresses. But in this case human intelligence and not soulless machinery was the propulsive force of reaction. The speculators had begun to work before the onward movement had come to an end or even begun to slacken. They were loaded up with a vast amount of stocks whose value, even if there had been money to redeem them, was severely limited, whereas they had purchased at prices varying between the first rise above nominal value and that reached by the last desperate speculator. It is not wise to hold such inflated stock too long, and in a crisis sailing-master Wisdom orders Quarter-master Caution to take a trick at the helm. When the bare idea of unification of financial interests was mooted, the wise holders of stock commenced to unload. When this movement began its progress was rapid—so long as there was anything to be moved. The first class to feel it were the bankers. The specie ran out like the pent-up water from a burst reservoir, till in an incredibly short time there was not sufficient remaining to afford the money-change needed in daily life. The advisers and officials of the State, seriously alarmed, began at once to take strong measures supported by royal decrees. Then as ruin began to stare the whole nation in the face more and more with every hour, desperate expedients were resorted to. The value of the currency was made by every stratagem, dishonest trick, and unscrupulous exercise of power, to fluctuate so that such differences or margins as arose might be grasped forthwith for national use. Payments in bullion, except for very small amounts, were forbidden. The possession of anything over five hundred livres in specie was deemed an offence punishable by confiscation, partial or wholesale, and by fine. Domiciliary visits were paid to seek evidence of offence and to enforce the new laws, and informers in this connection were well paid.

Then began a war, between public oppression and individual trickery, to defend acquired rights and evade unjust demands. The holders of paper money, unable to realise in specie, tried to protect themselves by purchasing goods of intrinsic value. Precious metals, jewels, and such like were bought in such quantities that the supplies diminished and the prices grew, until to avoid immediate ruin, such purchases were proclaimed illegal and prohibited. Then ordinary commodities of lesser values were tried as means of barter, till their prices too rose to such an extent that trade was paralysed. In order to meet the growing danger a still more desperate expedient was resorted to. A decree was issued the effect of which would be to reduce—gradually it was hoped—the obligation of bank notes to one-half their nominal value. This completed the panic, for here was a position which could not be guarded against by any prudence or wisdom.

No one could henceforth by any possibility be financially safe. The speculators who had already realised were alone safe. *Bona fide* investors, if not already overwhelmed by disaster, saw the tide of ruin rising rapidly around them. Nothing within the power of the state could now be done to check or even lessen the state of panic; not even the reversal of the late decree in ten days after its issue. To make matters still worse the Banque at this very time suspended payment. Probably in a wild endeavour to do *something* which would avert odium from itself by saddling the responsibility on someone else, the Government procured the dismissal of Law from the Controller-Generalship of Finance. However—strange to say—he was very soon appointed by the Regent as Intendant-General of Commerce and Director of the ruined bank. The much-vaunted, idolised, and believed-in "System" had now fallen hopelessly and was ruined forever. Law was everywhere attacked and insulted with such unmitigated rancour that he had to leave the country. He had invested the bulk of the great fortune which he had by now acquired, in estates in France; and these together with everything else that he had were now confiscated.

At the end of the same year, 1720, whilst he was at Brussels he was asked by the command of the Czar (Peter), to administer the finances of Russia, but declined. After this episode, grateful to a broken man, he spent a couple of years wandering about Italy and Germany and probably gaining a fluctuating income through gambling. Next he was to be found in Copenhagen where he had sought sanctuary from his creditors. Next year there was an outward change in his status, when he went to England, on a ship of war, at the invitation of the Government. There he was presented to George I. Somewhat to his chagrin he was denounced in the House of Lords as a Catholic—(he had abjured his old belief of Protestantism before accepting the high office of Controller-General of Finances in 1720)—and an adherent of the Pretender. He pleaded in the King's Bench the Royal pardon for the murder of Beau Austin which had been sent to him in 1719. He spent the succeeding few years in England whence he corresponded with the Duke of Orleans. He expected to be recalled to France but his hope was never realised. He wished to go to the Continent but was practically a prisoner in England, fearing to leave it lest he should be arrested by his creditors, amongst whom was the new French East India Company which had been reconstructed on the ruins of the old. In 1725 Sir Robert Walpole, then Prime Minister, asked Lord Townshend, the Secretary of State, to give Law a King's commission of some sort, so that such might serve for his protection. In the same year he went to Italy. He died in Venice in 1729, in what, compared with his former state, was poverty. To the last he was a gambler, always ready to take long risks for a prospect, however remote, of large gain. A story is told that in his last years he wagered his last thousand pounds to a shilling (20,000 to 1) against the throwing of double sixes six consecutive times. The law of chances was with him and naturally he won. He renewed his wager but the authorities would not allow the further gamble to take place.

John Law married, quite early in life, the daughter of the Earl of Banbury and widow of Mr. Seignior. His widow died in 1747. Some of the members of his family were not undistinguished; his son died a Colonel in the Austrian service; and one of his nephews became Comte de Lauriston and rose to be a General in the French army and Aide-de-Camp to the first Napoleon. He was made a Marshal of France by Louis XVIII.

John Law was a handsome and distinguished-looking man, blonde, with small dark grey eyes and fresh complexion. He made an agreeable impression on strangers. Saint-Simon, the social historian, gave him a good character: "innocent of greed and knavery, a mild good man whom fortune had not spoilt." Others of his time regarded him as a pioneer of modern statesmanship.

How is it then that such a man must be set down an impostor? In historical perspective as an impostor he must be regarded, though not as such in the narrowest view. The answer is that his very prominence sits amongst his judges. Lesser men, and greater men of lesser position, might well stand excused in matters wherein he is accorded condemnation.

> "That in the Captain's but a choleric word
> Which in the soldier is flat blasphemy."

If, when a man plays a game wherein life and death and the fortunes of many thousands are involved, it behoves him to be at least careful, much greater is his responsibility where the prosperity and happiness of nations are at stake. Had Law merely started new theories of finance, and had they gone wrong, he might well claim, and be accorded, excuse. But his were inventions of what, in modern slang, is called "get-rich-quick" principles. Not only did Law not enrich human life—with one exception, that of enlarging the currency in use—or add to the sum total of human well-being and happiness; he even neglected to show that forethought and consideration for others which in all honour ought to be exercised by the deviser and controller of great risks. He was a gambler, and a gambler only. He merely put into the pockets of some persons that which he had taken out of the pockets of others; and in doing so showed no consideration for the poor, the thrifty, the needy—for any of those whose contentment and happiness depend on such as are in high places and dowered in some way with productive powers. The soulless uneducated churl who does an honest day's work does more for humanity than the genius who merely shifts about the already garnered wealth of ages. John Law posed as a benefactor and accepted all the benefits that accrued to him from the praises of those who followed in his wake and gleaned the rich wastage of his empire-moving theories and schemes. Financiers of Law's type no more benefit a country or enrich a people than do the hordes of wasters and "tape"-betting men who prey on labour as locusts do on the crops. If they wish not to do unnecessary harm—which is putting their duty at the lowest possible estimate—they should at least try to avoid repeating the errors which have wrecked others. A brief glance at the wreckage which lay well within the Scotch gambler's vision, will show how he shut his eyes deliberately not only to facts, but to the many correlations of cause and effect. Before his Mississippi Scheme was formulated, there had been experience of banking enterprises, of schemes for mercantile combination and for the exploitation of capital, of adventurous dealings in the developments of countries new and more or less savage, East and West and South.

The following list will typify. Of all these John Law had knowledge sufficient to judge of difficulties to be encountered in the early stages, of dangers not only incidental to the things themselves, but based deep in human nature.

The East India Company founded in 1600
The Bank of England founded in 1694
The Africa Company founded in 1695
The Darien Company founded in 1695

A glance at each of these, all of which were within the scope and knowledge of Law, their aims, formation and development, up to the time spoken of, can hardly fail to be illuminative. The sixteenth century had been an age of adventure and discovery; the seventeenth of the foundation of great commercial enterprise, of conception of ideas, of the constructive beginnings of things. The time for development had come with the eighteenth; and now care and forethought, prudence and resource, were the preparations for success.

The East India Company was in reality the pioneer of corporate trading, and as for nearly a hundred years it was in a measure alone in its scale of magnitude, its experiences could well serve as exemplar, guide, and danger signal. It was based on that surest of all undertakings, natural growth. It came into existence because it was wanted, and from no other cause. Its very name, its modest capital, its self-protective purpose make for understanding.

In its Charter of Incorporation its purpose was indicated in the name: "The Governor and Company of Merchants of London trading to the East Indies." Its capital was £70,000, which though a large sum for those days, was, according to our modern lights, an almost ridiculously small sum for the object then before it, and to which it ultimately attained. The time was ripe for just such an undertaking.

The Peace of Vervins (1598) which left both France and Spain free to look after their domestic concerns, was immediately followed by the Edict of Nantes (1599) which gave religious liberty to France, and such a new freedom is always followed by national expansion. By this time Spain—the explorer or conqueror—and Holland—the patient organiser—held Eastern commerce in their hands. England had been gradually making a commerce of her own in the Indies, and all that was required was an official acknowledgment, so that the thunder of her guns should, when required, follow the creaking of her cordage. From the story of this great enterprise, through its first twenty-five years, could be drawn the lesson of such schemes as Law was now formulating. Though it had succeeded, in spite of Dutch and Portuguese opposition, in establishing "factories" when the historic massacre by the Dutch at Amboyna in the Molucca Islands, took place in 1725, the Eastern Company seemed near its dissolution. It was not till the establishment of the Hooghly factory in 1742 that things began to look up. After that, fortune favoured the Company more than she had appeared likely to do at the start. The marriage of Charles II to

Catherine of Braganza in 1661 brought progress in its train. Catherine's dower, which included Bombay and so put a part of Portugal's later possessions in British keeping, greatly stimulated the East India Company which thenceforth was able to weather the storms that threatened or assailed. The privilege of making war on its own account, conceded by Charles II, gave the Company a national importance which was destined to consolidate its interests with those of England itself. So strong did it become that before the end of the eighteenth century it was able to resist the attack on its charter made by a powerful and progressive rival, the "New Company." The rivals, after a few years of *pourparlers* and tentative efforts, were united in 1708; and thenceforth the amalgamation, under the title "The United Company of Merchants of England trading to the East Indies," was practically unassailable on its own account. It was additionally safe in that it had the protection of the great Whig Party under Godolphin. The capital of the Company, now enlarged to £3,200,000, was lent to the Government at five per cent. interest and was finally merged in the National Funds. The history of the Company, after 1717 does not belong here, as it is only considered as showing that John Law had the experience of an earlier Company similar to his own to guide him in its management if he had chosen to avail himself of it.

The Bank of England was, strangely enough,

the project of a Scotchman, William Paterson. The plan was submitted to Government in 1691 but was not carried into existence for three years. It was purely a business concern, brought into effective existence through the needs of commerce, the opportunity afforded being the need of the State and the concern of the statesman. It had a capital at first of over £1,200,000, which was loaned to the nation on the security of the taxes when the Charter was signed, there being certain safeguards against the possibility of political misuse. The Controlling Board was to have twenty-five members who were to be elected annually by the stockholders with a substantial qualification. There were at this time in England private banks; but this was an effort to formulate the banking rights, duties, and powers of capital under the ægis of the State itself. But even so sound a venture, enormously popular from the very first and with the whole might of the nation behind it, had its own difficulties to encounter. Its instantaneous success was an incentive to other adventurers; and the co-operation with government which it made manifest created jealousy with private persons and commercial concerns. Within two years its very existence was threatened, first by the individual hostility of those in the bullion trade, who already acted as bankers, and then by a rival concern incorporated under strong political support. This was the National Land Bank whose purpose was to use the security of real estate as a guarantee for the paper money which it issued for convenient usage. Strong as the Bank of England was by its nature, its popularity, and its support, it was in actual danger until the rival which had never "caught on"—to use an apposite Americanism—actually and almost instantaneously collapsed.

The safety thus temporarily obtained was purchased at the cost to the Government of a further loan of two million sterling—with the value to the contra of an alliance thus begun with the Whig ministry.

A further danger came from the mad and maddening South Sea Scheme five years later; but from which it was happily saved solely through the greater cupidity and daring of the newer company.

The Darien Company, which followed hard on the heels of The African Company, was formed in 1695, by Paterson; on the base of An Act of the Scottish Parliament for the purpose of making an opening for Scottish capital after the manner of the East India Company by which English enterprise had already so largely benefited. Its career was of such short duration and its failure so complete that there was little difficulty in understanding the causes of its collapse. It might serve for a *pendant* of Lamb's criticism of the meat that was "ill fed and ill killed, ill kept and ill cooked." The Company was started to utilise, in addition to exploiting new lands, the waste of time, energy and capital, between West and East; and yet it was not till the first trading fleet was sailing that its objective was made known to the adventurers. Its ideas of trading were those of a burlesque, and its materials of barter with tropical savages on the criminal side of the ludicrous—bibles, heavy woollen stuffs and periwigs! Naturally a couple of years finished its working existence and "The rest is silence." And yet at the inception of the scheme two great nations vied with one another for its control.

There are those who may say that John Law was not an impostor, but a great financier who made a mistake. Financiers must not make mistakes—or else they must be classed amongst the impostors; for they deal with the goods and prospects of others as well as their own. Law was simply a gambler on a great scale. He led a nation, through its units, to believe that the following of his ideas would lead to success. Financial schemes without good ideas and practical working to carry them out are deceptive and destructive. The Mississippi Scheme is a case in point. If the original intention had been carried out in its entirety—which involved vast pioneering and executive action of present and future generations, and an almost absolute foregoing of immediate benefits—the result would have been of immense service to the successors in title of the original ventures. The assessable value of the real estate conveyed under the Mississippi Scheme to-day equals more than a third of the present gigantic National Debt of France, swollen though the latter is by the Napoleonic wars, the war with Austria, the cost and indemnity of the war with Germany, and, in addition, by the long wars with England and Russia.

If human beings had been angels, content with the prospect of gains in the distant future, Law's schemes might have succeeded. As it was, he, working for his own purposes with an imperfect humanity, can only be judged by results.

WITCHCRAFT AND CLAIRVOYANCE

A. THE PERIOD

FOR convenience, the masculine offender is in demonology classed under the female designation. According to Michelet and other authorities there were ten thousand alleged witches for each alleged wizard! and anyhow there is little etiquette as to the precedence of ladies in criminal matters.

The first English Statute dealing directly with witches appears to be the thirty-third of Henry VIII (1541) which brought into the list of felonies persons "devising or practising conjurations, witchcraftes, sorcerie or inchantments or the digging up of corpses," and depriving such of the benefit of clergy. It was however repealed by I Edward VI Cap. 12, and again by I Mary (in its first section.). Queen Elizabeth, however, passed another Act (5 Elizabeth Cap. 16) practically repeating that of her father, which had been in abeyance for more than thirty years. The Statute of Elizabeth is exceedingly interesting in that it states the condition of the law at that time. The opening words leave no misunderstanding:

"Whereas at this day there is no ordinary nor condigne punishment provided against the wicked offences of conjurations or invocations of evil spirits, or of sorceries, inchantments, charmes or witchcraftes, which be practised to the distruction of the persons and goods of the Queene's subjects, or for other lewd purposes. Be it enacted that if any person or persons after the first day of June next coming, shall use practice, or exercise any invocations, or conjurations, of evill or wicked spirits, to or for any intent or purpose, or else if any person or persons after the said first day of June shal use, practice or exercise any witchcraft, enchantment, charme or sorcerie, whereby any person shall happen to be killed or destroied, that then as well every such offendour or offendours in invocations, or conjurations, as is aforesayde, their aydours and counsellors, as also everie such offendour or offendours in that Witchcrafte, enchantment, charme or sorcerie whereby the death of any person doth ensue, their ayders and counsellors, being of eyther of the sayde offences lawfully convicted and attainted, shall suffer paines of death, as a felon or felons, and shall lose the privilege and benefit of Clergy and sanctuary," &c.

In this act lesser penalties are imposed for using any form of witchcraft or sorcery, for inducing to any persons harm, or to "provoke any person to unlawfull love or to hurt or destroy any person in his or her bodye, member or goods," or for the discovery or recovery of treasure. From that time down to the first quarter of the eighteenth century, when the law practically died out, witchcraft had its place in the category of legal offences. The law was finally repealed by an Act in the tenth year of George II. The sixteenth and seventeenth centuries were the time of witch-fever, and in that period, especially in its earlier days when the belief had become epidemic, it was ruthless and destructive. It is said that in Genoa five hundred persons were burned within three months in the year 1515, and a thousand in the diocese of Como in a year. Round numbers in such matters are to be distrusted, as we find they seldom bear investigation; but there is little doubt that in France and Germany vast numbers suffered and perished. Even in more prosaic and less emotional England there were many thousands of judicial murders in this wise. It is asserted that within two centuries they totalled thirty thousand.

It is startling to find such a weird and impossible credulity actually rooted in the Statute book of one's own country, and that there are records of judges charging juries to convict. Sir Matthew Hale, a great lawyer, a judge of the Common Pleas in 1654, and Lord Chief Justice in 1671, was a firm believer in witchcraft. He was a grave and pious man, and all his life was an ardent student of theology as well as of law. And yet in 1664 he sentenced women to be burned as witches. In 1716 a mother and daughter—the latter only nine years of age—were hanged in Huntingdon. In Scotland the last case of a woman being condemned as a witch occurred at Dornoch in 1722.

It is no easy task in these days, which are rationalistic, iconoclastic and enquiring, to understand how the commonalty not only believed in witchcraft but acted on that belief. Probably the most tolerant view we can take, is that both reason and enquiry are essential and rudimentary principles of human nature. Every person of normal faculties likes to know and understand the reasons of things; and inquisitiveness is not posterior to the period of maternal alimentation. If we seek for a cause we are bound to find one—even if it be wrong. *Omne ignotum pro magnifico* has a wide if not always a generous meaning; and when fear is founded on, if not inspired by ignorance, that unthinking ferocity which is one of our birthrights from Adam is apt to carry us further than we ever meant to go. In an age more clear-seeing than our own and less selfish we shall not think so poorly of primitive emotions as we are at present apt to. On the contrary we shall begin to understand that in times when primitivity holds sway, we are most in touch with the loftiest things we are capable of understanding, and our judgment, being complex, is most exact. Indeed in this branch of the subject persons used to call to aid a special exercise of our natural forces—the æsthetic. When witchcraft was a belief, the common idea was that that noxious power was almost entirely held by the old and ugly. The young, fresh, and beautiful, were seldom accepted as witches save by the novelty-loving few or those of sensual nature. This was perhaps fortunate—if the keeping down of the population in this wise was necessary; it is easier as well as safer to murder the uncomely than those of greater charm. In any case there was no compunction about obliterating the former class. The general feeling was much the same as that in our own time which in sporting circles calls for the destruction of vermin.

It will thus be seen that the profession of witchcraft, if occasionally lucrative, was nevertheless always accompanied with danger and execration. This was natural enough since the belief which made witchcraft dangerous was based on fear. It is not too much to say that in every case, professed witchcraft was an expression of fraudulent intent. Such pity, therefore, as the subject allows of must be confined to the guiltless victims who, despite blameless life, were tried by passion, judged by frenzy, and executed by remorseless desperation. There could be no such thing as quantitative analysis of guilt with regard to the practice of witchcraft: any kind of playing with the subject was a proof of *some* kind of wrongful intent, and was to be judged with Draconian severity. Doubtless it was a very simple way of dealing with evils, much resembling the medical philosophy of the Chinese. The whole logic of it can be reduced to a sorites. Any change from the normal is the work of the devil—or *a* devil as the case may be. Find out the normal residence of that especial devil —which is in some human being. Destroy the devil's dwelling. You get rid of the devil. It is pure savagery of the most primitive kind. And it is capable of expansion, for logic is a fertile plant, and when its premises are wrong it has the fecundity of a weed. Before even a savage can have time to breathe, his logic is piling so fast on him that he is smothered. If a human being is a devil then the club which destroys him or her is an incarnation of good, and so a god to be worshipped in some form—or at any rate to be regarded with esteem, like a sword, or a legal wig, or a stethoscope, or a paint-brush, or a shovel, or a compass, or a drinking-vessel, or a pen. If all the necessary conditions of life and sanity and comfort were on so primitive a base, what an easy world it would be to live in!

One benefit there was in witchcraft, though it was not recognised officially as such at the time. It created a new industry—a whole crop of industries. It is of the nature of belief that it encourages belief—not always of exactly the same kind—but of some form which intelligence can turn into profit. We cannot find any good in the new industry—grapes do not grow on thorns nor figs on thistles. The sum of human happiness was in no sense augmented; but at least a good deal of money or money's worth changed hands; which, after all, is as much as most of the great financiers can point to as the result of long and strenuous success. In the organisation of this form of crime there were many classes, of varying risks and of benefits in inverse ratio to them. For the ordinary rule of finance holds even here: large interest means bad security. First there were the adventurers themselves who took the great risks of life and its collaterals—esteem, happiness, &c. The money obtained by this class was usually secured by fraudulent sales of worthless goods or by the simple old financial device of blackmail. Then there were those who were in reality merely parasites on the pleasing calling—those timorous souls who let "'I dare not' wait upon 'I would' like the poor cat i' the adage." These were altogether in a poorer way of trade than their bolder brothers and sisters. They lacked courage, and sometimes even sufficient malice for the proper doing of their work; with the result that success seldom attended them at all, and never heartily. But at any rate they could not complain of inadequate punishment; whenever religious zeal flamed up they were generally prominent victims. They can in reality only be regarded as specimens of parasitic growth. Then there came the class known in French criminal circles as *agents provocateurs*, whose business was not only to further ostensible crime but to work up the opposition against it. Either branch of their art would probably be inadequate; but by linking their services they managed to eke out a livelihood. Lastly there was the lowest grade of all, the Witch-finder —a loathly calling, comparable only to the class or guild of "paraskistae" or "rippers" in the ritual of the Mummy industry of ancient Egypt.

Of these classes we may I think consider some choice specimens—so far as we may fittingly investigate the *personnel* of a by-gone industry. Of the main body, that of Wizards and Witches or those pretending to the cult, let us take Doctor Dee and Madame Voisin, and Sir Edward Kelley and Mother Damnable—thus representing the method of the procession of the unclean animals from the Ark. Of the class of Witchfinders one example will probably be as much as we can stand, and we will naturally take the one who obtained fame in his calling—namely Matthew Hopkins, who stands forth like Satan, "by merit raised to that bad eminence."

B. DOCTOR DEE

EVEN a brief survey of the life of the celebrated "Doctor Dee," the so-called "Wizard" of the sixteenth century, will leave any honest reader under the impression that in the perspective of history he was a much maligned man. If it had not been that now and again he was led into crooked bye-paths of alleged occultism, his record might have stood out as that of one of the most accomplished and sincere of the scientists of his time. He was in truth, whatever were his faults, more sinned against than sinning. If the English language is not so elastic as some others in the matter of meaning of phrases, the same or a greater effect can be obtained by a careful use of the various dialects of the British Empire. In the present case we may, if English lacks, well call on some of the varieties of Scotch terminology. The intellectual status of the prime wizard, as he is held to be in general opinion, can be well indicated by any of the following words or phrases "wanting," "crank," "a tile off," "a wee bit saft," "a bee in his bonnet." Each of these is indicative of some form of monomania, generally harmless. If John Dee had not had some great qualities, such negative weaknesses would have prevented his reputation ever achieving a permanent place in history of any kind. As it is his place was won by many accomplished facts. The following is a broad outline of his life, which was a long one lasting for over eighty years.

John Dee was born in 1527, and came of a Welsh race. A good many years after his start in life he, after the harmless fashion of those (and other) times, made out a family tree in which it was shewn that he was descended from, among other royalties, Roderick the Great, Prince of Wales. This little effort of vanity did not, however, change anything. The world cared then about such things almost as little as it does now; or, allowing for the weakness of human beings in the way of their own self-importance, it might be better to say as it professes to do now. John Dee was sent to the University of Cambridge when he was only fifteen years old. The College chosen for him was St. John's, and here he showed extraordinary application in his chosen subject, mathematics. He took his probationary degree of Bachelor of Arts in 1545, and was made a Fellow in 1546. In his early years of College life his work was regulated in a remarkable way. Out of the twenty-four hours, eighteen were devoted to study, four to sleep, the remaining two being set apart for meals and recreation. Lest this should seem incredible it may be remembered that three hundred years later, the French Jesuits, having made exhaustive experiments, arrived at the conclusion that for mere purposes of health, without making any allowance for the joy or happiness of life, and treating the body merely as a machine from which the utmost amount of work mental and physical could be got without injury, four hours of sleep per diem sufficed for health and sanity. And it is only natural that a healthy and ambitious young man trying to work his way to success would, or might have been, equally strenuous and self-denying. His appointment as Fellow of St. John's was one of those made when the College was founded. That he was skilled in other branches of learning was shown by the fact that in the University he was appointed as Under Reader in Greek. He was daring in the practical application of science, and during the representation of one of the comedies of Aristophanes, created such a sensation by appearing to fly, that he began to be credited by his companions with magical powers. This was probably the beginning of the sinister reputation which seemed to follow him all his life afterwards. When once an idea of the kind has been started even the simplest facts of life and work seem to gather round it and enlarge it indefinitely. So far as we can judge after a lapse of over three hundred years, John Dee was an eager and ardent seeker after knowledge; and all through his life he travelled in the search wherever he was likely to gain his object. It is a main difficulty of following such a record that we have only facts to follow. We know little or nothing of motives except from results, and as in the development of knowledge the measure of success can only bear a small ratio to that of endeavour, it is manifest that we should show a large and tolerant understanding of the motives which animate the seeker for truth. In the course of his long life John Dee visited many lands, sojourned in many centres of learning, had relations of common interests as well as of friendship with many great scholars, and made as thinker, mathematician, and astronomer, a reputation far transcending any ephemeral and purely gaseous publicity arising from the open-mouthed wonder of the silly folk who are not capable of even trying to understand things beyond their immediate ken. Wherever he went he seems to have been in touch with the learned and progressive men of his time, and always a student. At various times he was in the Low Countries, Louvain (from whose University he obtained the degree of LL.D.), Paris, Wurtemberg, Antwerp, Presburg, Lorraine, Frankfort-on-the-Oder, Bohemia, Cracow, Prague, and Hesse-Cassel. He even went so far afield as St. Helena. He was engaged on some great works of more than national importance. For instance, when in 1582, Pope Gregory XIII instituted the reform of the Calendar which was adopted by most of the great nations of the world, Dee approved and worked out his own calculations to an almost similar conclusion, though the then opposition to him cost England a delay of over one hundred and seventy years. In 1572 he had proved his excellence as an astronomer in his valuable work in relation to a newly discovered star (Tycho Brahe's) in Cassiopœia. In 1580 he made a complete geographical and hydrographical map of the Queen's possessions. He tried—but unhappily in vain—to get Queen Mary to gather the vast collections of manuscripts and old books which had been made in the Monasteries (broken up by Henry VIII) of which the major part were then to be obtained both easily and cheaply. He was a Doctor of Laws (which by the way was his only claim to be called "Doctor" Dee, the title generally accorded to him). He was made a rector in Worcestershire in 1553; and in 1556, Archbishop Parker gave him ten years' use of the livings of Upton and Long Leadenham. He was made Warden of Manchester College in 1595, and was named by Queen Elizabeth as Chancellor of St. Paul's. In 1564, he was appointed Dean of Gloucester, though through his own neglect of his own interest it was never carried out. The Queen approved, the Archbishop sealed the deed; but Dee, unmindful, overlooked the formality of acceptance and the gift eventually went elsewhere. Queen Elizabeth, who consistently believed in and admired him, wanted to make him a bishop, but he declined the responsibility. For once the formality at consecration: "*Nolo Episcopari*" was spoken with truthful lips. More than once he was despatched to foreign places to make special report in the Queen's service. That he did not—always, at all events—put private interest before public duty is shown by his refusal to accept two rectories offered to him by the Queen in 1576, urging as an excuse that he was unable to find time for the necessary duties, since he was too busily occupied in making calculations for the reformation of the Calendar. He seems to have lived a most proper life, and was twice married. After a long struggle with adversity in which—last despair of a scholar—he had to sell his books, he died very poor, just as he was preparing to migrate. At his death in 1608 he left behind him no less than seventy-nine works —nearly one for each year of his life. Just after the time of the Armada, following on some correspondence with Queen Elizabeth, he had returned to England after long and adventurous experiences in Poland and elsewhere, during which he had known what it was to receive the honours and affronts of communities. He took back with him the reputation of being a sorcerer, one which he had never courted and which so rankled in him that many years afterwards he petitioned James I to have him tried so that he might clear his character.

If there be any truth whatever in the theory that men have attendant spirits, bad as well as good, Dr. Dee's bad spirit took the shape of one who pretended to occult knowledge, the so-called Sir Edward Kelley of whom we shall have something to say later on.

Dee was fifty-four years of age when he met Sir Edward Kelley who was twenty-eight years his junior. The two men became friends, and then the old visionary scholar at once became dominated by his younger and less scrupulous companion, who very soon became his partner. From that time Dee's down-fall—or rather down-*slide* began. All the longings after occult belief which he had hitherto tried to hold in check began not only to manifest themselves, but to find expression. His science became merged in alchemy, his astronomical learning was forced into the service of Astrology. His belief, which he as a cleric held before him as a duty, was lost in spiritualism and other forms of occultism. He began to make use for practical purposes of his crystal globe and his magic mirror in which he probably had for long believed secretly. Kelley practically ruined his reputation by using for his own purposes the influence which he had over the old man. His opportunities were increased by the arrival in England of Laski, about 1583. The two scholars had many ideas in common, and Kelley did not fail, in the furtherance of his own views, to take advantage of the circumstance. He persuaded Dee to go with his new friend to Poland, in the hope of benefiting further in his studies in the occult by wider experience of foreign centres of learning. They journeyed to Laskoe near Cracow, where the weakness of the English scholar became more evident and his form of madness more developed. Dee had now a fixed belief in two ideas which he had hitherto failed to materialise—the Philosopher's Stone and the Elixir of Life, both of them dreams held as possible of realisation to the scientific dreamer in the period of the Renaissance. Dee believed at one time that he had got hold of the Philosopher's Stone, and actually sent to Queen Elizabeth a piece of gold taken from a transmuted warming-pan. As it is said in the life of Dee that he and Kelley had found a quantity of the Elixir of Life in the ruins of Glastonbury Abbey, we can easily imagine what part the latter had in the transaction. It was he, too, who probably fixed on Glastonbury as the place in which to search for Elixirs, as that holy spot had already a reputation of its own in such matters. It has been held for ages that the staff used by Joseph of Arimathea took root and blossomed there. Somehow, whatever the Glastonbury Elixir did, the Philosopher's Stone did not seem to keep its alleged properties in the Dee family. John Dee's young son Arthur, aged eight, tried its efficacy; but without success. Perhaps it was this failure which made Kelley more exacting, for a couple of years later in 1589, he told his partner that angels had told him it was the divine wish that they should have their wives in common. The sage, who was fond of his wife—who was a comely woman, whereas Kelley's was ill favoured and devoid of charms—naturally demurred at such an utterance even of occult spirits. Mrs. Dee also objected, with the result that there were alarums and excursions and the partnership was rudely dissolved—which is a proof that though the aged philosopher's mind had been vitiated by the evil promptings of his wily companion he had not quite declined to idiocy.

C. LA VOISIN

IN Paris a woman named Des Hayes Voisin, a widow who had taken up the business of a midwife, towards the end of the seventeenth century made herself notorious by the telling of fortunes. Such at least was the manifest occupation of the worthy lady, and as she did not flaunt herself unduly, her existence was rather a retired one. Few who did not seek her services knew of her existence, fewer still of her residence. The life of a professor of such mysteries as the doings of Fate—so-called—is prolonged and sweetened by seclusion. But there is always an "underground" way of obtaining information for such as really desire it; and Madame Voisin, for all her evasive retirement, was always to be found when wanted—which means when she herself wanted to be found. She was certainly a marvellous prophet, within a certain range of that occult art. Like all clever people she fixed limitations for herself; which was wise of her, for to prophesy on behalf of every one who may yearn for a raising of the curtain, be it of never so small a corner, on all possible subjects, is to usurp the general functions of the Almighty. Wisely therefore, Madame Voisin became a specialist. Her subject was husbands; her chief theme their longevity. Naturally such women as were unsatisfied with the personality, circumstances, or fortunes of their partners, joined the mass of her *clientèle,* a mass which taking it "bye and large" maintained a strange exactness of dimensions. This did not much trouble the public, or even the body of her clients, for no one except Madame herself knew their numbers. It was certainly a strange thing how accurately Madame guessed, for she had seemingly no data to go on—the longevity of the husbands were never taken into the confidence of the prophet. She took care to keep almost to herself the rare good fortune, in a sense, which attended her divination; for ever since the misfortune which had attended the late Marquise de Brinvilliers became public, the powers of the law had taken a quite unnecessary interest in the proceedings of all of her cult. Longevity is quite a one-sided arrangement of nature; we can only be sure of its accuracy when it is too late to help in its accomplishment. In such a game there is only one throw of the dice, so that it behoves anyone who would wager successfully to be very sure that the chances are in his—or her—favour.

Madame Voisin's clients were generally in a hurry, and so were willing to take any little trouble or responsibility necessary to ensure success. They had two qualities which endear customers to those of La Voisin's trade; they were grateful and they were silent. That they were of cheery and hopeful spirit was shown by the fact that as a rule they married again soon after the dark cloud of bereavement had fallen on them. When the funeral baked meats have coldly furnished forth the marriage tables, it is better to remain as inconspicuous as possible; friends and onlookers will take notice, and, when they notice, they will talk. Moreover the new partner is often suspicious and apt to be a little jealous of his predecessor in title. Thus, Madame Voisin being clever and discreet, and her clients being—or at any rate appearing to be—happy in their new relations and silent to the world at large, all went prosperously with the kindly-hearted prophet. No trouble rose as to testamentary dispositions. Men who are the subjects of prophecy have usually excellently-drawn wills. This is especially the case with husbands who are no longer young. Young husbands are as a rule not made the subjects of prophecy.

Madame Voisin's great accuracy of prediction did not excite at the time so much public admiration as it might have done if she or her clients had taken the public more into their confidence; but it was noted afterwards that in most cases the male individual who retired early from the scene was the senior partner in that *congeries* of three which has come to be known as "the eternal triangle." In later conversations, following in the wake of the completed prophecy, confidences were exchanged as to the studies in certain matters of science in which Madame Voisin seemed to have attained a rare proficiency.

The late Mr. Charles Peace, an adventurous if acquisitive spirit, who gave up his life in the same manner as the deceased Mr. Haman, worked alone during the long period of his professional existence, and with misleading safety. The illustrious French lady-prophet unwisely did not value this form of security, and so multiplied opportunities of failure. She followed an entirely opposite policy, one which though it doubtless stood by her on many occasions had a fatal weakness. In some ways it may facilitate matters if one is one's own Providence; such a course avoids temporarily errors of miscalculation or deduction of probable results. And just as the roulette table has certain chances in favour of Zero, there is for the practical prophet a large hazard in that the dead are unable to speak or to renew effort on a more favourable basis. La Voisin, probably through some unfavourable or threatening experiences, saw the wisdom of associating the forces of prediction and accomplishment, and with the readiness of an active personality effected the junction. For this she was already fairly well equipped with experiences. Both as a wife and a lover of warm and voluptuous nature she understood something of the passions of humanity, on both the female and the male side; and being a woman she knew perhaps better of the two the potency of feminine longing. This did not act so strongly in the lesser and more directly commercial, if less uncertain, phases of her art, such as finding lost property, divining the result of hazards, effecting immunity from danger, or the preserving indefinitely the more pleasing qualities of youth. But in sterner matters, when the issue was of life or death, the masculine tendency towards recklessness kicked the beam. As a nurse in active touch with both medical and surgical wants, aims, and achievements, she was at ease in the larger risks of daily life. And after all, her own ambitions, aided by the compelling of her own natural demands for physical luxury, were quite independent, only seeking through exiguous means a way of achievement. In secret she studied the mystery of a toxicologist; and, probably by cautious experiment, satisfied herself of her proficiency in that little-known science. That she had other aims, more or less dependent on this or the feelings which its knowledge superinduced, can be satisfactorily guessed from some of her attendant labours which declared themselves later.

After a time La Voisin's vogue as a sorceress brought her into certain high society where freedom of action was unhampered by moral restraints. The very rich, the leaders of society and fashion of the time, the unscrupulous whose ambitious efforts had been crowned with success of a kind, leaders of Court life, those in high military command, mistresses of royalty and high aristocracy—all became companions and clients in one or more of her mysterious arts. Amongst them were the Duchesse de Bouillon, the Comtesse de Soissons, Madame de Montespan, Olympe de Mancini, Marshal de Luxembourg, the Duc de Vendôme, Prince de Clermont-Lodeve. It was not altogether fashionable not to be in touch with Madame Voisin. Undeterred by the lessons of history, La Voisin went on her way, forced as is usual in such cases by the circumstances which grow around the criminal and prove infinitely the stronger. She was at the height of her success when the public suspicion, followed by action, revealed the terrible crimes of the Marquise de Brinvilliers; and she was caught in the tail of the tempest thus created.

This case of Madame de Brinvilliers is a typical one of how a human being, goaded by passion and lured by opportunity, may fall swiftly from any estate. It is so closely in touch with that of Madame Voisin that the two have almost to be considered together. They began with the desire for dabbling in forbidden mysteries. Three men—two Italians and one German, all men of some ability—were violent searchers for the mythical "philosopher's stone" which was to fulfil the dream of the mediæval alchemist by turning at will all things into gold. In the search they all gravitated to Paris. There the usual thing happened. Money ran short and foolish hoping had to be supplemented by crime. In the whirling world of the time there was always a ready sale for means to an end, however nefarious either might be. The easy morality of the time allowed opportunity for all means, with the result that there was an almost open dealing in poisons. The soubriquet which stole into existence—it dared not proclaim itself—is a self-explanatory historical lesson. The *poudre de succession* marks an epoch which, for sheer, regardless, remorseless, profligate wickedness is almost without peer in history, and this is said without forgetting the time of the Borgias. Not even natural affection or family life or individual relationship or friendliness was afforded any consideration. This phase of crime, which was one almost confined to the upper and wealthier classes, depended on wealth and laws of heredity and entail. Those who benefited by it salved what remnants of conscience still remained to them with the thought that they were but helping the natural process of waste and recuperation. The old and feeble were removed, with as little coil as might be necessary, in order that the young and lusty might benefit. As the change was a form of plunder, which had to be paid for in a degree in some way approximate to results, prices ran high. Poisoning on a successful scale requires skilful and daring agents, whose after secrecy as well as whose present aid has to be secured. Exili and Glasser—one of the Italians and the German—did a thriving trade. As usual in such illicit traffic, the possibility of purchase under effective conditions made a market. There is every reason to believe from after results that La Voisin was one such agent. The cause of La Brinvilliers entering the market was the purely personal one of an affair of sensual passion. Death is an informative circumstance. Suspicion began to leak out that the polyglot firm of needy foreigners had dark dealings. Two of them—the Italians—were arrested and sent to the Bastille where one of them died. By unhappy chance the other was given as cell-companion Captain Sainte-Croix, who was a lover of the Marquise de Brinvilliers. Sainte-Croix as a Captain in the regiment of the Marquis had become intimate in his house. Brinvilliers was a fatuous person and of imperfect moral vision. The Captain was handsome, and Madame la Marquise amorous. Behold then all the usual *personnel* of a tragedy of three. After a while the intrigue became a matter of family concern. The lady's father,—the Civil Lieutenant d'Aulroy, procured a *lettre de cachet,* and had the erring lover immured in the Bastille as the easiest and least public way out of the difficulty. "Evil communications corrupt good manners," says the proverb. The proverbial philosopher understated the danger of such juxtaposition. Evil manners added corruption even to their kind. In the Bastille the exasperated lover listened to the wiles of Exili; and another stage of misdoing began. The Marquise determined on revenge, and be sure that in such a case in such a period even the massive walls of the Bastille could not prevent the secret whisper of a means of effecting it. D'Aulroy, his two sons, and another sister perished. Brinvilliers himself was spared through some bizarre freak of his wife's conscience. Then the secret began to be whispered —first, it was said, through the confessional; and the *Chambre Ardente,* analogous to the British Star Chamber, instituted for such purposes, took the case in hand. The result might have been doubtful, for great social forces were at work to hush up such a scandal, but that, with a truly seventeenth century candour, the prisoner had written an elaborate confession of her guilt, which if it did not directly assure condemnation at least put justice on the right track.

The trial was a celebrated one, and involved incidentally many illustrious persons as well as others of lesser note. In the end, in 1676, Madame la Marquise de Brinvilliers was burned—that is, what was left of her was burned after her head had been cut off, a matter of grace in consideration of her rank. It is soothing to the feelings of many relatives and friends—not to mention those of the principal—in such a case when "great command o'ersways the order" of purgation by fire.

Before the eddy of the Brinvilliers' criminal scandal reached to the lower level of Madame

Voisin, a good many scandals were aired; though again "great command" seems to have been operative, so far as human power availed, in minimising both scandals and punishments. Amongst those cited to the *Chambre Ardente* were two nieces of Cardinal Mazarin, the Duchesse de Bouillon, the Comtesse de Soissons, and Marshal de Luxembourg. In some of these cases that which in theatrical parlance is called "comic relief" was not wanting. It was a witty if impertinent answer of the Duchesse de Bouillon to one of her judges, La Reyne, an ill-favoured man, who asked, apropos of a statement made at the trial that she had taken part in an alleged invocation of Beelzebub, "and did you ever see the Devil?"—

"Yes, I am looking at him now. He is ugly, and is disguised as a Councillor of State!"

The King, Louis XIV, took much interest in the trial and even tried now and again to smooth matters. He even went so far as to advise the Comtesse de Soissons who was treated by the Court rather as a foolish than a guilty woman, to keep out of the way if she were really guilty. In answer she said with the haughtiness of her time that though she was innocent she did not care to appear in a Law Court. She withdrew to Brussels where she died some twenty years later. Marshal de Luxembourg—François Henri de Montmorenci-Boutteville, duke, peer, Marshal of France to give his full titles—was shown to have engaged in an attempt to recover lost property by occult means. On which basis and for having once asked Madame Voisin to produce his Satanic Majesty, he was alleged to have sold himself to the Devil. But his occult adventures did not stand in the way of his promotion as a soldier though he had to stand a trial of over a year long; he was made Captain of the Guard and finally given command of the Army.

La Voisin with her accomplices—a woman named Vigoureux and Le Sage, a priest—were with a couple of score of others arrested in 1679, and were, after a spell of imprisonment in the Bastille, tried. As a result Voisin, Vigoureux and her brother, and Le Sage were burned early in 1680. In Voisin's case the mercy of previous decapitation, which had been accorded to her guilty sister Brinvilliers, was not extended to her. Perhaps this was partly because of the attitude which she had taken up with regard to religious matters. Amongst other unforgivable acts she had repelled the Crucifix—a terrible thing to do according to the ideas of that superstitious age.

D. SIR EDWARD KELLEY

CARLYLE in his *French Revolution* makes a contrast between two works of imagination which mark the extremes of the forces that made for the disruption of France, *Paul et Virginie* and *Le Chevalier de Faublas*. The former he calls "the swan-song of old dying France"; of the latter he says "if this wretched *Faublas* is a death-speech, it is one under the gallows, and by a felon that does not repent." This double analogy may well serve for a comparison of Dr. Dee and the man who was at once his partner for a time, and his evil genius. The grave earnest old scholar, with instincts for good, high endeavour, and a vast intellectual strength, contrasts well with the mean-souled shifty specious rogue who fastened himself on him and leech-like drained him "dry as hay."

Such historians as mention the existence of the latter are even a little doubtful how to spell his name. This, however, does not matter much—nay, at all, for it is probably not that to which he was born. Briefly the following is his record as far as can be discovered. He was born in 1555 to parents living in Worcester, who having tried to bring him up as an apothecary, sent him to Oxford when he was seventeen years of age. There he was entered at Gloucester Hall, under the name of Talbot. As however three men of that name were in the Hall at the same time, it is doubtful what family can claim the honour of his kinship. His college life was short—only lasting a year—and inconspicuous. "He left," we are told, "abruptly." Then, as if to complete the purely educational phase of his existence, he was for a while an attorney, eking out the tenuity of his legal practice by aid of forgery. Thus full-fledged for his work in life, he made his first properly-recorded appearance in the pillory in 1580, for an offence which is variously spoken of as forgery and coining. At any rate his ears were cropped off, a loss which necessitated for prudential reasons his wearing a skullcap for the remainder of his days. This he wore with such conspicuous success that it is said that even Doctor Dee, who was his partner for nearly seven years, did not know of his mutilation. Kelley's next recorded offence was one which in a later age when subjects for dissection (necessary for purposes of education in anatomy) were difficult to obtain, was popularly known as "body-snatching." The commission of this offence though a serious breach of the law, came to be regarded as a necessary condition of study; and even if punishment was meted out, it was not looked upon as dishonour. But in Kelley's case the offence was committed not for the purpose of scientific education but for one of sorcery. It took place in Walton-le-dale in Lancashire, where Kelley dug up a body buried on the previous day, for purposes of necromancy, which, it will be remembered, was, as the etymology of the word implies, divination by means of the dead.

From this time on, he seemed to see his way clear to the final choice of a profession. He had tasted crime and punishment, and considered himself well qualified to accept the risks as well as the benefits; and so chose fraud as his life work. He was still under twenty-five years of age when he began to look about him for his next means or occasion of turning his special talents to profit. After some deliberation he fixed on the existence and qualities of the famous (as he had then become) Doctor Dee, and carefully commenced operations. He called on the mathematician at his house at Mortlake and made his acquaintance. Dee was naturally impressed by the conversation and ostensible qualities of the young man, who had the plausibility of the born rogue and laid himself out to captivate the old man, more than double his companion's age and worn by arduous study. He fostered all Dee's natural weaknesses, humoured his fads, was enthusiastic regarding his beliefs which he appeared to share, and urged on his personal ambitions. The belief in occultism which the philosopher cherished in secret, though he had openly and formally repudiated it a dozen years before in his preface to

Sir Henry Billingsley's translation of Euclid, gave the parasitic rogue his cue for further ingratiating himself, and before long he entered Dee's service at an annual salary of fifty pounds. His special function was that of "skryer," which was his own or Dee's reading of "seer." His contribution to the general result was to see the figures which did—or did not—appear in the so-called "magic" crystal, an office for which his useful imagination, his unblushing assurance, and his utter unscrupulousness eminently fitted him. In fact he was in his designs of fraud a perfect complement of the simple-minded scientist. Of course as days went on and opportunities offered themselves, through Dee's growing madness and Kelley's social enlargements, the horizon of chicanery widened. This was largely assisted by the opportune arrival in England of the Palatine Albert Laski in 1583. Laski was just the man that Kelley was waiting for. A rich man with a taste for occult science; sufficiently learned to keep in touch with the theories of occultism of that time; sufficiently vain to be used by an unscrupulous adventurer who tickled his intellectual palate whilst he matured his frauds upon him.

Kelley having worked on Dee's feelings sufficiently to secure his acquiescence, procured that Laski should be allowed to aid in such operations and experiments as appealed to him. The result was that the Palatine took the two men with him, promising a free field for them both, each according to his bent. At Prague, in 1583, Laski presented Dee and his companion to the Emperor Rudolph II. Encouraged by the royal approval, Dee looked for a longer sojourn in eastern Europe, and brought thither his wife and children from Poland, where he had left them at Laskoe, the seat of the Palatine. Later on, in 1585,—again through the influence of the credulous Laski—Dee with his companion was presented to Stephen, King of Poland. Stephen was much interested, and attended a *séance* that he might see the spirits of which he had heard so much. He saw too much, however, as far as Kelley was concerned, for he penetrated the imposture. Thereupon Kelley, unequal to carrying on the business single-handed, for he dared not let Dee's eyes be opened and he knew he could not induce him to be other than a blind partner, contrived that a new confederate should be added to the firm. This was one Francis Pucci, a Florentine, possessed of all the address and subtlety of his race. But after the experience of a year he was removed on suspicion of bad faith. Before that year was out, the Bishop of Piacenza, Apostolic Nuncio at the Emperor's Court, had a decree issued that the two Englishmen should quit Prague within six days. From Prague they went to Erfurt, in Thuringia; but despite letters of recommendation from high quarters the Municipal Authorities would not allow them to remain. So they moved on to Hesse-Cassel and thence to Tribau in Bohemia, where the fraud of making spirits appear was renewed. In 1586, it was intimated to Dee that the Emperor of Russia wished to receive him in that country. He would receive a fee of two thousand pounds per annum and would be treated with honour; but the scholar did not see his way to accept the flattering offer. At Tribau, Kelley experimented, but unsuccessfully, with some powder found at Glastonbury, Dee's young son being the medium. It was noticeable that whenever Dee or his family failed in these experiments, Kelley always succeeded. At this stage Kelley, who was a man of evil life, fell madly in love with Dee's wife.. He was married himself, but that did not seem to matter. His own wife was ugly and unattractive, whereas the second Mrs. Dee was well-favoured and winning. In the madness of his lust he tried to work on the husband's credulity by telling him that it had been conveyed to him through angels that it was the Divine wish that the two men should hold their wives in common. Dee was naturally sceptical and annoyed, and his wife was furious. Kelley, however, was persistent, and stuck to his point so stedfastly that after a while the woman's resolution began to give way, and for a time some sort of working arrangement came about. Kelley's story, as elaborated to his partner, was that at Tribau, in 1587, the crystal showed him a vision of a naked woman who conveyed to him the divine message. To Dee's unhinged mind this seemed all natural and correct—probably even to the suitable costume adopted by the angelic messenger: so the worthy doctor gave way. After a time however the matron recovered her sanity, and the vulture and the pigeon parted. Dee gave up to his late partner all the "tools of trade" and "properties" of the fraud, and the two never met again.

Kelley went to Prague where he was thrown into prison in 1589. He remained in durance for four years after which he was released. From thence on till 1595, he became a vagabond as well as a rogue, and wandered about Germany. He again fell into the hands of Rudolph, to be again imprisoned by him. He was killed whilst making a desperate effort to escape.

There seems to be no record of Edward Kelley—or Talbot—having been knighted, no authority save his own wish for the use of the title. It may of course be possible that he was knighted by the Emperor in some moment of absurd credulity; but there is no record of it. He had no children.

E. MOTHER DAMNABLE

OWING to a want of accord among historians, the searcher after historic truth in our own day can hardly be quite sure of the identity of the worthy lady who passed under the above enchanting title. To later generations the district of Camden Town—formerly a suburb of London but now a fairly central part of it—is best known through a public house, the *Mother Red-Cap*. But before controversy can cease we are called on to decide if Mother Red-Cap and Mother Damnable were one and the same person. A hundred years ago a writer who had made such subjects his own, came to the conclusion that the soubriquet Mother Damnable was synonymous with Mother Black-Cap whom he spoke of as of local fame. But in the century that has elapsed historical research has been more scientifically organised and the field from which conclusions can be drawn has been enlarged as well as explored. The fact is that a century ago the northern suburb had two well-known public houses, *Mother Red-Cap* and *Mother Black-Cap*. It is possible that both the worthy vintners who offered "entertainment for man and beast" meant one and the same person, though who that person was remains to be seen. The distinctive colour line of the two hostelries was also possibly due to considerations of business rather than of art. *Red-cap* and *Black-cap* are, as names, drawn from these varying sign-boards; the term *Mother* held in common is simply a title given without any pretence of doing honour to the alleged practices of the person whom it is intended to designate.

There were in fact two notorious witches, either of whom might have been in the mind of either artistic designer. One was of Yorkshire fame in the time of Henry VII. The other was of very much later date and of purely local notoriety. The two publicans who exploited these identities under pictorial garb were open and avowed trade rivals. The earlier established of the two had evidently commissioned a painter to create a striking sign-board on a given subject, and the artist had fulfilled his task by an alleged portrait of sufficiently fearsome import to fix the attention of the passer-by, at the same time conveying to him some hint of the calling of the archetype on which her fame was based. Prosperity in the venture begot rivalry; and the owner of the new house of refreshment, wishing to outshine his rival in trade whilst at the same time availing himself of the publicity and local fame already achieved, commissioned another artist to commit another pictorial atrocity under the name of art. So far as the purpose of publicity went, the ideas were similar; the only differences being in the colour scheme and the measure of attractiveness of the alleged prototype. From the indications thus given one may form some opinion —based solely on probability—as to which was the earlier and which the later artistic creation, for it is by this means—and this means only—that we may after the lapse of at least a century bring tradition to our aid, and guess at the original of Mother Damnable.

Of the two signs it seems probable that the black one is the older. After all, the main purpose of a sign-board is to catch the eye, and unless Titian and all who followed him are wrong, red has an attractive value beyond all other hues. The dictum of the great Italian is unassailable: "Red catches the eye; yellow holds it; blue gives distance." A free-souled artist with the choice of the whole palette open to him might choose black since historical accuracy was a matter to be valued; but in a question of competition a painter would wisely choose red—especially when his rival had confined himself to black. So far as attractiveness is concerned, it must be borne in mind that the object of the painter and his patron was to bring customers to a London suburban public house in the days of George III. To-day there is a cult of horrors in Paris which has produced some choice specimens of decorative art, such for instance as the café known as *Le Rat Mort*.

Such places lure their customers by curiosity and sheer horror; but the persons lured are from a class dominated by "Gallic effervescence" and attracted by anything that is *bizarre,* and not of the class of the stolid beer-drinking Briton. But even the most stolid of men is pleased by the beauty of a woman; so the sign-painter—who knows his art well, and has evolved from the ranks of his calling such a man as Franz Hals—we may be sure, when he wished to please, took for his model some gracious personality.

Now the artist of the lady of dark headgear let his imagination run free and produced a face typical of all the sins of the Decalogue. We may therefore take it on the ground of form as well as that of colour that priority of date is to be given to Mother Black-Cap. There is good ground for belief that this deduction is correct. Naturally the owner of the earliest public-house wished to make it as attractive as possible; and as Camden Town was a suburb through which the northern traffic passed on its way to and from London, it was wise to use for publicity and entertainment names that were familiar to north country ears. Before the railways were organised the great wheeled and horse-traffic between London and the North—especially Yorkshire which was one of the first Counties to take up manufacturing and had already most of the wool trade—went through Camden Town. So it was wise forethought to take as an inn sign a Yorkshire name. The name of Mother Shipton had been in men's mouths and ears for about two hundred years, and as the times had so changed that the old stigma of witchcraft was not then understood, the association of the name with Knaresborough alone remained. And so Mother Shipton of Knaresborough was intended as the prototype of the inn portrait with black head-gear at Camden Town. In the ordinary course of development and business one of the two inns succeeded and lasted better than the other. And as Mother Red-Cap has as a name supplanted Mother Damnable, we may with some understanding discuss who that lady was.

She was a well-known shrew of Kentish Town, daughter of one Jacob Bingham, a local brick-maker, who had married the daughter of a Scotch pedlar manifestly not of any high moral character as shown by her later acts and the general mistrust which attended them. They had one daughter, Jinny, who in wickedness outdid her parents. She was naturally warm-blooded and had a child when she was sixteen by a man of no account, George Coulter, known as Gipsy George. Whatever affection may have existed between them was cut short by his arrest—and subsequent execution at Tyburn —for sheepstealing. In her second quasi-matrimonial venture Jinny lived a cat-and-dog life with a man called Darby who spent his time in getting drunk and trying to get over it. Number Two's end was also tragic. After a violent quarrel with his companion he disappeared. Then there was domestic calm for a while, possibly due to the fact that Bingham and his wife were being tried also on a charge of witchcraft, complicated with another capital charge of procuring the death of a young woman. They were both hanged and thereafter Jinny found time for another episode of love-making and took up with a man called Pitcher. He too disappeared, but his body, burned almost to a cinder, was discovered in a neighbouring oven. Jinny was tried for murder, but escaped on the plea that the man often took refuge in the oven when he wished to get beyond reach of the woman's venomous tongue, to which fact witness was borne by certain staunch companions of Miss Bingham.

Jinny's third venture towards happy companionship, though it lasted much longer, was attended with endless bitter quarrelling, and came to an equally tragic end, had at the beginning a spice of romance. This individual, whose name has seemingly not been recorded, being pursued in Commonwealth times for some unknown offence, had sought her aid in attempting to escape. This she had graciously accorded, with the consequence that they lived together some years in the greatest unhappiness.

At length he died—of poison, but by whom administered did not transpire at the inquest. For the rest of her life Miss Bingham, who was now old, lived under the suspicion of being a witch. Her ostensible occupation was as a teller of fortunes and a healer of odd diseases—occupations which singly or together make neither for personal esteem or general confidence. Her public appearances were usually attended by hounding and baiting by the rabble; and whenever anything went wrong in her neighbourhood the blame was, with overt violence of demeanour, attributed to her. She did not even receive any of the respect usually shown to a freeholder—which she was, having by her father's death become owner of a house which he had built for himself with his own hands on waste ground. Her only protector was that usual favourite of witches, a black cat, whose devotion to her and whose savage nature, accompanied by the public fear shown for an animal which was deemed her "familiar," caused the mob to flee before its appearance.

The tragedy and mystery of her life were even exceeded by those of her death. When, having been missed for some time, her house was entered she, attended only by her cat and with her crutch by her side, was found crouching beside the cold ashes of her extinct fire. In the tea-pot beside her was some liquid, seemingly brewed from herbs. Willing hands administered some of this to the black cat, whose hair, within a very short time, fell off. The cat forthwith died. Then the clamour began. Very many people suddenly remembered having seen, after her last appearance in public, the Devil entering her house. No one, however, had seen him come out again. What a pity it was that no veracious scribe or draughtsman was present in the crowd which had noticed the Devil's entry to the house. In such case we might have got a real likeness of His Satanic Majesty—a thing which has long been wanted—and the opportunities of obtaining which are few.

One peculiar fact is recorded of Madame Damnable's burial; her body was so stiff from the *rigor mortis*—or from some other cause—that the undertakers had to break her limbs before they could put her body in the coffin.

F. MATTHEW HOPKINS

THERE is one thing more evil than oppression in the shape of wrong-doing, and that is oppression in the guise of good. Tennyson, in one of his poems, speaks of the dishonest pharmacist who "pestles a poison'd poison." This is a refinement of iniquity; a poisoned poison is not even an enlargement of evil but a structural change eliminating the intention of good and replacing it with evil intent. Witches were quite bad enough; or rather they would have been, had that which was alleged of them been true. But a man who got his living by creating suspicion regarding them and following it out to the practical consummation of a hideous death, was a thousand times worse. To-day such a functionary as a witch-finder exists, it is true; but only amongst the very lowest and most debased savages. And it is only by the recorded types made known to us that it is possible even to guess at the iniquity of their measures, the vileness of their actions. In the full tally of the two centuries during which the witch mania existed in England, it is impossible to parallel the baseness of the one man who distinguished himself in this loathsome occupation. The facts of his history speak for themselves. Matthew Hopkins was born in Suffolk early in the seventeenth century. He was the son of a minister, James Hopkins of Wenham. He was brought up for the law, and when enrolled as an attorney, practised in Ipswich; but after a while he moved to Manningtree where, after he had given up the law, he took to the calling of witch-finder, being the first person in England to follow that honourable trade.

If he had had no suitable opportunities of earning an honest livelihood and been graced with no education, some excuse might have been offered for his despicable calling. But when we remember that he passed his youth in a household practising religion, and was a member of a learned profession, it is difficult to find words sufficiently comprehensive for the fit expression of our natural indignation against him. If picturesque profanity were allowable, it might be well applied to this despicable wretch and his nefarious labours. In no imaginable circumstances could there possibly be anything to be said in mitigation of his infamy. When we think that the whole ritual of oppression was in his own hands—that he began with lying and perjury, and ended with murder; that he showed, throughout, ruthless callousness for the mental and physical torture of great numbers of the most helpless class of the community, the poor, the weak, the suffering, the helpless and hopeless; that when once his foul imagination had consecrated any poor wretch to destruction, or his baleful glance had unhappily lighted on some unsuspecting victim there was for such only the refuge of death, and that by some means of prolonged torture, we cannot find any hope or prospect even in evil dreams of the nether world, of any adequate punishment for his dreadful sins. When we remember that this one man—if man he can be called—was in himself responsible for what amounted to the murder of some two hundred women whom he pursued to the death, the magnitude of his guilt can be guessed but not realised.

He occupied three whole years in his fell work; and in those years, 1644, 1645 and 1646, he caused a regular reign of terror throughout the counties of Huntingdon, Norfolk, Suffolk and Essex. He had a gang of his own to help him in his gruesome work of "discovering" witches; amongst whom was a wretch called John Stern and—to her shame—a woman, whose name is unrecorded. These three had a sort of mock assize of their own. They made regular tours of discovery, at a charge of twenty shillings for expenses at each place they visited. There appears to have been a fee paid or exacted for each witch "bagged"; and such was his greed that after a while he actually lowered the price. In 1645, which was perhaps his "best" year, the price declined to a shilling a head. Hopkins and his gang took comfort, however, from the fact that the industry was a growing one. The trade had only been initiated in 1644, and already in a year's time he had in one day procured the execution of eighteen alleged witches; and at the end of that assize, after the gaol delivery had been effected, one hundred and twenty suspects still awaited trial. In the skilful hands of Matthew Hopkins, trial was only a step on the road to certain execution by one of the forms in use. Here came in, not only the witchfinder's legal knowledge, but also his gift of invention—the latter being used in the formulation of so-called "tests" which were bound to be effective. Of these the simplest was the water test. The subject's thumbs were tied together and she was then thrown into water of sufficient depth. If she did not drown, it was taken as a proof of guilt; and she was hanged by form of law. In some cases, as an alternative, she was burned. If she did not stand the test her friends had the pleasure of knowing that she was pronounced to have died innocent. In any case there was no further trouble with her. Such was the accuracy as well as the simplicity of similar "tests" that, in the twenty years previous to the Restoration, between three and four thousand alleged witches perished in England from one cause or another. Hopkins professed to be both just and merciful. He seemed generally willing to afford a "test" to the accused; though, truth to tell, the result was always the same. In such cases the test was eminently calculated to evoke confession, and such confession, no matter how ridiculous or extravagant it might be, was simply a curved road to the rope or the torch instead of a straight one. One of these pleasing "tests" was to place the old woman—they were all women and all old—sitting cross-legged on a stool or table where she could be well watched. She was generally kept in that position under inspection, without food or water, for twenty-four hours. At the end of that time such resolution as had remained disappeared, and in the vain blind hope of some change for the better, some alleviation however slight of the grinding misery, of the agony of body and mind and soul, they confessed. And such confessions! The very consideration of such of them as now remain in the cold third-person method of a mere recorder, almost makes one weep; there is hardly a word that is not almost a certificate of character. With every desire to confess—for such was the last hope of pleasing their torturers—their utter ignorance of confessional matter is almost a proof of innocence.

Just imagine the scene—a village or hamlet, or the poorer quarter of a small country town with squalid surroundings, marking a poverty which in this age has no equal; a poor, old, lonely woman whose long life of sordid misery, of hunger and the diseases that huddle closely around want, hopeless, despairing, recognising her fate through the prolonged physical torture with which age and infirmity rendered her unable even to attempt to cope. Round her gathered, in a sickly ring, a crowd of creatures debased by the exercise of greed and cruelty to a lower level than the beasts. Their object is not to inquire, to test, to judge; but only to condemn, to wreck, to break, to shatter. Some of them, she realises even in her agony, are spurred on by the same zeal which animated the cruelty of followers of Ignatius in the grim torture-chambers of the Inquisition.

The poor dazed, suffering old creature, racked with pains prolonged beyond endurance, tries to rally such glimmerings of invention as are possible to her untaught, unfed mind; but finds herself at every failure fluttering helplessly against a wall of spiritual granite which gives back not even an echo to her despairing cry. At last she comes to that stage where even fright and fear have no standing room, and where the blank misery of suffering ceases to be effective. Then the last flicker of desire for truth or rectitude of purpose dies away, and she receives in feeble acquiescence such suggestions as are shouted or whispered to her, in the hope that by accepting them she may win a moment's ease of body or mind, even if it be her last on earth. Driven beyond mortal limits her untutored mind gives way; and with the last remnants of her strength she yields her very soul to her persecutors. The end does not matter to her now. Life has no more to offer her—even of pain, which is the last conscious tie to existence. And through it all, ghoul-like, watching and waiting for the collapse, whilst outwardly he goes through the mechanical ritual of prayer, we see in the background the sinister figure of the attorney, preparing in his mind such evidence as he may procure or invent for his work of the next day.

It needs the imagination of a Dante to consider what should be the place of such an one in history, and any eternity of punishment that that imagination could suggest must be inadequate. Even pity itself which rests on sympathy and is kin to the eternal spirit of justice, would have imagined with satisfaction the wretched soul going through a baleful eternity clinging in perpetual agony of fear to the very King of Terrors.

In judging Matthew Hopkins one must not, in justice to others, accord him any of the consideration which is the due of good intent. Not a score of years after his shameful death, a man was born in a newer land far beyond the separating sea, who through his influence, his teaching, the expression of his honest conviction, was the cause of perhaps more deaths than the English anti-witch. We refer to Cotton Mather, who believed he wrought for the Lord—in his own way—in New England. But guilt does not attach to him. He was an earnest, though mistaken man, and the results of his mistaken teaching were at variance with the trend of his kindly, godly life.

It must be pleasing to the spirit of the Old Adam which is in us all in some form, to think of the manner of the death of Matthew Hopkins. Three years had exhausted not only the material available for his chosen work, but, what was worse for him, the patience of the community. Moreover, he had given cause for scandal in even his own degraded trade and in himself, the filthiest thing in connection with it. Not content with dealing with the poor, helpless folk, whom he had come to regard as his natural prey, he went on fancy flights of oppression. At last he went too far. He ventured to denounce an aged clergyman of blameless life. The witch-fever was too strong for justice in any form, and neither age, high character, nor sacred office could protect this gentleman of eighty years of age. He too was tortured, till in a moment of unhinged mind, he confessed as he was ordered, and was duly hanged. This was in 1645. The old man's death was not in vain, for it was made the occasion of much necessary plain speaking. Presently the public conscience was wakened; chiefly by another cleric, the Rev. John Caule, vicar of Great Staughton, Huntingdonshire—all honour to him!—who, though strange to say he believed in witchcraft, realised the greater evil wrought by men like Hopkins. He published a pamphlet in which he denounced Hopkins as a common nuisance. The result, if slow, was sure. The witch-finder never recovered from the shock of Caule's vigorous attack. In 1647, on information based on Hopkins' own rules, he was arrested and subjected to the test which he had devised: he was tied by the thumbs and thrown into the water. Unfortunately for himself he withstood the test—drowning, except for a short period of pangs, is an easy death—and so was by process of Law duly hanged.

One can imagine how the whole atmosphere of the country—surcharged with suspicion, fear, oppression, torture, perjury or crime—was cleared by the execration which followed the removal of this vile wretch.

VI. ARTHUR ORTON

(The Tichborne Claimant.)

IN the annals of crime, Arthur Orton, the notorious claimant to the rich estates and title of Tichborne, takes a foremost place; not only as the originator of one of the most colossal attempts at fraud on record, but also from his remarkable success in duping the public. It would be difficult indeed to furnish a more striking example of the height to which the blind credulity of people will occasionally attain. Of pretenders, who by pertinacious and unscrupulous lying have sought to bolster up fictitious claims, there have been many before Orton; but he certainly surpassed all his predecessors in working out the lie circumstantial in such a way as to divide the country for years into two great parties—those who believed in the Claimant, and those who did not. Over one hundred persons, drawn from every class, and for the most part honest in their belief, swore to the identity of this illiterate butcher's son —this stockman, mail-rider and probably bushranger and thief—as the long-lost son and heir of the ancient house of Tichborne of Titchborne. To gain his own selfish ends this individual was ready to rob a gentlewoman of her fair fame, to destroy the peace of a great family who, to free themselves from a persecution, as cruel as it was vicious, had to be pilloried before a ruthless and unsympathising mob, to have the privacy of their home invaded, and to hear their women's names banded from one coarse mouth to another. Thus, and through no fault of their own, they were compelled to endure a mental torture far worse than any physical suffering, besides having to expend vast sums of money, as well as time and labour, in order to protect themselves from the would-be depredations of an unscrupulous adventurer. It has been estimated that the resistance of this fictitious claim cost the Tichborne estate not far short of one hundred thousand pounds.

The baronetcy of Tichborne, now Doughty-Tichborne, is one of the oldest. It has been claimed that the family held possession of the Manor of Tichborne for two hundred years before the Conquest. Be this as it may—and, in the light of J. H. Round's revelations, some scepticism as to these pre-Norman pedigrees is permissible—their ancestors may be traced back to one Walter de Tichborne who held the manor, from which he took his name, as early as 1135. Their names too, are interwoven with the history of the country. Sir Benjamin, the first baronet—for the earlier de Tichbornes were knights,—as Sheriff of Southhampton, on the death of Queen Elizabeth, re-

Photo. by Maull & Fox. Copyright.

ARTHUR ORTON

paired instantly to Winchester and on his own initiative proclaimed the accession of James VI of Scotland as King of England, for which service he was made a baronet, and his four sons received the honour of knighthood. His successor, Sir Richard, was a zealous supporter of the Royal cause during the civil wars. Sir Henry, the third baronet, hazarded his life in the defence of Charles I and had his estates sequestered by the Parliamentarians though he was recompensed at the Restoration.

Believers in occultism might see in the trials and tribulations brought down upon the unfortunate heads of the Tichborne family by the machinations of the Claimant, the realisation of the doom pronounced by a certain Dame Ticheborne away back in the days of Henry II.

Sir Roger de Ticheborne of those days married Mabell, the daughter and heiress of Ralph de Lamerston, of Lamerston, in the Isle of Wight, by whom he acquired that estate. This good wife played the part of lady bountiful of the neighbourhood. After a life spent in acts of charity and goodness, as her end drew nigh and she lay on her death bed, her thoughts went out to her beloved poor. She begged her husband, that in order to have her memory kept green the countryside round, he would grant a bequest sufficient to ensure, once a year, a dole of bread to all comers to the gates of Tichborne. To gratify her whim Sir Roger promised her as much land as she could encompass while a brand plucked from the fire should continue to burn. As the poor lady had been bedridden for years her husband may have had no idea that she could, even if she would, take his promise seriously. However, the venerable dame, after being carried out upon the ground, seemed to regain her strength in a miraculous fashion, and, to the surprise of all, managed to crawl round several rich and goodly acres which to this day are known as "the Crawls."

Carried to her bed again after making this last supreme effort and summoning her family to her bedside, Lady Ticheborne predicted with her dying breath, that, as long as this annual dole was continued, so long should the house of Tichborne prosper; but, should it be neglected, their fortunes would fail and the family name become extinct from want of male issue. As a sure sign by which these disasters might be looked for, she foretold that a generation of seven sons would be immediately followed by one of seven daughters.

The benevolent custom thus established was faithfully observed for centuries. On every Lady Day crowds of humble folk came from near and far to partake of the famous dole which consisted of hundreds of small loaves. But ultimately the occasion degenerated into a noisy merry-making, a sort of fair, until it was finally discontinued in 1796, owing to the complaints of the magistrates and local gentry that the practice encouraged vagabonds, gipsies and idlers of all sorts to swarm into the neighbourhood under pretence of receiving the dole.

Strangely enough Sir Henry Tichborne, the baronet of that day (the original name of de Tiche-borne had by this time been reduced to Tichborne), had seven sons, while his eldest son who succeeded him in 1821, had seven daughters. The extinction of the family name, too, came to pass, for in the absence of male issue, Sir Henry, the eighth bar-onet, was succeeded by his brother, who had taken the surname of Doughty on coming into the estates bequeathed to him on these terms, by a distant rela-tive, Miss Doughty; though, in after years, his brother, who in turn succeeded him, obtained the royal licence to couple the old family name with that of Doughty. Following this repeated lapse of direct male heirs came other troubles; but it is to be hoped that the successful defeat of the fraudu-lent claim of Arthur Orton set a period to the doom pronounced long years ago by the Lady Mabell.

Most families, great and small, have their secret troubles and unpleasantness, and the Tichbornes seem to have had their share of them. To this may be traced the actual, if remote, cause of the Claim-ant's imposture. James Tichborne, afterwards the tenth baronet, the father of the missing Roger, who was drowned in the mysterious loss of the *Bella,* off the coast of South America, in the spring of 1854, lived abroad for many years; but, while his wife was French in every sentiment, he himself from time to time exhibited a keen desire to return to his native land. When Roger was born there was small likelihood of his ever succeeding to either title or estates, and so his education was almost entirely a foreign one.

Sir Henry Tichborne, who had succeeded in 1821, though blessed with seven beautiful daughters, had no son. Still there was their uncle Edward, who had taken the name of Doughty, and he, after Sir Henry, was the next heir. Edward, too, had a son and daughter. But, one day, news came to James and his wife, in France, that their little nephew was dead; and with the possibilities which this change opened up, it brought home to the father the error he had committed in permitting Roger to grow up ignorant of the English tongue and habits. It was manifest that Mr. James F. Tichborne was not unlikely to become the next baronet, and he felt it his bounden duty to make good his previous neglect, by providing his son with an English education, such as would fit him for his probable position as head of the house of Tichborne. In this praiseworthy intention he met with strong opposition from his wife whose great aim it was to see her son grow up a Frenchman. To her, France was the only land worth living in. She cared nought for family traditions; her dream was that her darling boy should marry into some distinguished family in France or Italy. If he was to enter the army, then it should be in some foreign service. But to England he should not go if she could prevent it.

James Tichborne, like many weak men with self-willed wives, put off the inevitable day as long as he could; and in the end only achieved his purpose by strategy. Roger was sixteen years of age when news arrived of the death of Sir Henry. Naturally James arranged to be present at his brother's funeral and it was only reasonable that he should be accompanied by his son Roger, whom everyone now regarded as the heir. Accordingly the boy took leave of his mother, but under the solemn injunction to return quickly. However, his father had determined otherwise. After attending the funeral of his uncle, at the old chapel at Tichborne, Roger was, by the advice of relatives and friends, and with the consent of the boy himself, taken down to the Jesuit College at Stonyhurst. When Mrs. Tichborne learned of this step, her fury knew no bounds. She upbraided her husband violently; and there was a renewal of the old scenes in the Tichborne establishment. Roger wrote his mother filial, if ill-spelt, letters in French; but, for a year, the son, though ardently looking for a letter, got no token of affection from the incensed and indignant lady.

During his three years' stay at Stonyhurst, Roger seems to have applied himself diligently to the study of English; but, though he made fair progress, he was never able to speak it with as much purity and command of words as when conversing in French. In Latin, mathematics, and chemistry, too, he contrived to make fair headway; while his letters evidenced an inclination for the study of polite literature. If not highly accomplished, he was of a refined and sensitive nature. During this period he made many friends, spending his vacation with his English relatives in turn. His great delight was to stay at Tichborne, then in possession of his father's brother, Sir Edward Doughty. Withal, the shy, pale-faced boy steadily gained in favour, for he had a nature which disarmed ill-feeling. As time wore on it became necessary to determine on some profession for the lad; and needless to say his father's choice of the army added fuel to the fire of his wife's anger. After some delay a commission was obtained and Mr. Roger Charles Tichborne was gazetted a coronet in the Sixth Dragoons, better known as the Carbineers.

Defeated in her purpose of making a Frenchman of her boy, Roger's mother yet continued to harp upon her old desire to marry him to one of the Italian princesses of whom he had heard so much. But Roger had other ideas, for he had fallen passionately in love with his cousin—Miss Katharine Doughty afterwards Lady Radcliffe. However, the course of love was not to run smooth. The Tichbornes had always been Roman Catholic, and the marriage of first cousins was discountenanced by that church. Consequently when some little token incidentally revealed to the father the secret and yet unspoken love of the young people, their dream was rudely shattered.

That the girl warmly reciprocated her cousin's affection was beyond question, and Lady Doughty was certainly sympathetic though she took exception to certain of her nephew's habits. He was an inveterate smoker besides drinking too freely. These and other little failings seem to have aroused some fear in her anxious mother's heart, though she quite recognised the boy's kind disposition, and the fact that he was truthful, honourable and scrupulous in points of duty. Still she would not oppose the wishes of the young lovers—except to the extent of pleading and encouraging Roger to master his weaknesses. It was Christmas time in 1851 when the *dénoument* came and the eyes of Sir Edward were opened to what was going on. He was both vexed and angry, and was resolved that the engagement should be broken off before it grew more serious. One last interview was permitted to the cousins and, this over, the young man was to leave the house forever. The great hope of his life extinguished, there was nothing left for Roger but to rejoin his regiment, then expecting orders for India, and to endeavour to forget the past. Still even in those dark days neither Roger nor Kate quite gave up hope of some change. Lady Doughty, despite her dread of her nephew's habits, had a warm regard for him, and could be relied upon to plead his cause; and in a short time circumstances unexpectedly favoured him. Sir Edward was ill and, fearing that death was approaching, he sent for his nephew and revived the subject. He explained that if it were not for the close relationship he should have no objection to the marriage and begged Roger to wait for three years. If then the affection, one for the other, remained unaltered, and providing that Roger obtained his own father's consent and that of the Church, he would accept things as the will of God and agree to the union. As might be expected, Roger gratefully promised loyally to observe the sick man's wishes.

However, Sir Edward, instead of dying, slowly mended, and Roger returned to his regiment. Occasionally he would spend his leave with his aunt and uncle, when the young people loved to walk together in the beautiful gardens of Tichborne exchanging sweet confidences and weaving plans for the future. On what proved to be his last visit to his ancestral home, in the midsummer of 1852, Roger, to comfort his cousin, confided a secret to her—a copy of a vow, which he had written out and signed, solemnly pledging himself, in the event of their being married before three years had passed, to build a church or chapel at Tichborne as a thanks offering to the Holy Virgin for the protection shown by her in praying God that their wishes might be fulfilled.

His leave up, Roger went back to his regiment

more than ever a prey to his habitual melancholy. To his great regret the orders for the Carbineers to go to India were countermanded. He accordingly determined to throw up his commission and travel abroad until his period of probation had passed. South America had long been the subject of his dreams, and so thither he would make his way; and in travelling through that vast continent he hoped to find occupation for his mind and so get through the trying period of waiting. His plan was to spend a year in Chili, Guayaquil and Peru, and thence to visit Mexico, and so, by way of the United States, to return home. Having come to this resolution he lost no time in putting it into execution. Being of business-like habits he made his will, in which he purposely omitted any mention of the "church or chapel." This secret had already been committed to paper, and with other precious souvenirs of his love for his cousin, had been confided to his most trusted friend—Mr. Gosford, the steward of the family estate. After paying a round of farewell visits to his parents and old friends in Paris, Roger finally set sail from Havre, on March 21, 1853, in a French vessel named *La Pauline,* for Valparaiso, at which port she arrived on the 19th of the following June, when Roger set out on his wanderings. During his travels Roger continued to write home regularly; but the first news he received was bad. Sir Edward Doughty had died almost before the *Pauline* had lost sight of the English shores; and Roger's father and mother were now Sir James and Lady Tichborne.

Presently the wanderer began to retrace his steps, making his way to Rio de Janeiro. Here, he found a vessel called the *Bella* hailing from Liverpool, about to sail for Kingston, Jamaica, and as he had directed his letters and remittances to be forwarded there, he prevailed upon the captain to give him a passage. On the 20th of April, 1854, the *Bella* passed from the port of Rio into the ocean. From that day no one ever set eyes upon her. Six days after she left harbour, a ship traversing her path found, amongst other ominous tokens of a wreck, a capsized long-boat bearing the name "*Bella,* Liverpool."

These were taken into Rio and forthwith the authorities caused the neighbouring seas to be scoured in quest of survivors; but none were ever found. That the *Bella* had foundered there was little room to doubt. It was supposed that she had been caught in a sudden squall, that her cargo had shifted, and that, unable to right herself, the vessel had gone down in deep water, giving but little warning to those on board. In a few months the sad news reached Tichborne, where the absence of letters from the previously diligent correspondent had already raised grave fears. The sorrow-stricken father caused enquiries to be made in America and elsewhere. For a time, there was a faint hope that some one aboard the *Bella* might have been picked up by some passing vessel; but, as months wore on, even these small hopes dwindled away. The letters which poor Roger had so anxiously asked might be directed to him at the post office, Kingston, Jamaica, remained there till the ink grew faded; the banker's bill which lay at the agents' remained unclaimed. At last the unfortunate vessel was finally written off at Lloyd's as lost, the insurance money paid, and gradually the *Bella* faded from the memories of all but those who had lost friends or relatives in her. Lady Tichborne alone, refused to abandon hope.

Her obstinate disregard of such conclusive evidence of the fate of her unfortunate son preyed upon her mind to such an extent as to make her an easy victim for any scheming rascal pretending to have news of her lost son; and "sailors," who told all sorts of wild stories of how some of the survivors of the *Bella* had been rescued and landed in a foreign port, became constant visitors at Tichborne Park and profited handsomely from the weak-minded lady's credulity. Sir James, himself, made short work of these tramping "sailors," but after his death, in 1862, the lady became even more ready to be victimised by their specious lies.

Firm in her belief that Roger was still alive, Lady Tichborne now caused advertisements to be inserted in numerous papers; and in November, 1865, she learnt through an agency in Sydney that a man answering the description of her son had been found in Wagga Wagga, New South Wales. A long correspondence ensued, the tone and character of which ought to have put her on her guard; but, over-anxious to believe that she had indeed found her long-lost son, any wavering doubts she may have had, were swept from her mind by the evidence of an aged negro servant named Boyle, an old pensioner of the Tichborne family. Boyle, who lived in New South Wales, professed to recognise the Claimant as his dear young master, and he certainly remained one of his most devoted adherents to the end. Undoubtedly this man's simplicity proved a very valuable asset to Orton. His intimate knowledge of the arrangements of Tichborne Park was pumped dry by his new master, who, aided by a most tenacious memory, was afterwards able to use the information thus obtained with startling effect.

As to the identity of the Claimant with Arthur Orton there can be absolutely no doubt. As a result of the enquiries made by the trustees of the Tichborne estate nearly the whole of his history was unmasked. He was born, in 1834, at Wapping where his father kept a butcher's shop. In 1848 he took passage to Valparaiso, whence he made his way up country to Melipilla. Here he stayed some eighteen months receiving much kindness from a family named Castro, and it was their name he went under at Wagga Wagga. In 1851 he returned home and entering his father's business became an expert slaughterman. The following year he emigrated to Australia; but after the spring of 1854 he ceased to correspond with his family. He had evidently led a life of hardship and adventure—probably not unattended with crime, and certainly with poverty. At Wagga Wagga he carried on a small butcher's business, and it was from here that he got into communication with Lady Tichborne just after his marriage to an illiterate servant girl.

According to his subsequent confession, until his attention was drawn to the advertisement for the missing Roger, he had never even heard of the name of Tichborne, and it was only his success when, by way of a joke upon a chum, he claimed to be the missing baronet, that led him to pursue the matter in sober earnest. Indeed he seemed at first very reluctant to leave Australia, and probably he was only driven to accede to Lady Tichborne's request, to return "home" at once, by the fact that he had raised large sums of money on his expectations. His original intention was probably to obtain some sort of recognition, and then to return to Australia with whatever money he had succeeded in collecting.

After wasting much time he left Australia and arrived in England, by a very circuitous route, on Christmas Day, 1866. His first step on landing, it was subsequently discovered, was to make a mysterious visit to Wapping. His parents were dead, but his enquiries showed a knowledge, both of the Orton family and the locality, which was afterwards used against him with very damaging effect. His next proceeding was to make a flying and surreptitious excursion to Tichborne House, where, as far as possible, he acquainted himself with the bearings of the place. In this he was greatly assisted by one Rous, a former clerk to the old Tichborne attorney, who was then keeping a public house in the place. From this man, who became his staunch ally, he had no doubt acquired much useful information; and it is significant that he sedulously kept clear of Mr. Gosford, the agent to whom the real Roger had confided his sealed packet before leaving England.

Lady Tichborne was living in Paris at this time and it was here, in his hotel bedroom, on a dark January afternoon, that their first interview took place for, curiously enough, the gentleman was too ill to leave his bed! The deluded woman professed to recognise him at once. As she sat beside his bed, "Roger" keeping his face turned to the wall, the conversation took a wide range, the sick man showing himself strangely astray. He talked to her of his grandfather, whom the real Roger had never seen; he said he had served in the ranks; referred to Stonyhurst as Winchester; spoke of his suffering as a lad from St. Vitus's dance—a complaint which first led to young Arthur Orton being sent on a sea voyage; but did not speak of the rheumatism from which Roger had suffered. But it was all one to the infatuated woman—"He confuses everything as if in a dream," she wrote in exculpating him; but unsatisfactory as this identification was, she never departed from her belief. She lived under the same roof with him for weeks, accepted his wife and children, and allowed him £1,000 a year. It did not weigh with her that the rest of the family unanimously declared him to be an impostor, or that he failed to recognise them or to recall any incident in Roger's life.

Nearly four years elapsed before the Claimant commenced his suit of ejectment against the trustees of the infant Sir Alfred Tichborne—the posthumous son of Roger's younger brother; but he utilised the time to good purpose. He had taken into his service a couple of old Carbineers who had been Roger's servants and before long so completely mastered small details of regimental life that some thirty of Roger's old brother-officers and men were convinced of his identity. He went everywhere, called upon all Roger's old friends, visited the Carbineers' mess and generally left no stone unturned to get together evidence in support of his identity. As a result of his strenuous activity and plausibility he produced at the first trial over one hundred witnesses who, on oath, identified him as Roger Tichborne; and these witnesses included Lady Tichborne, the family solicitor, magistrates, officers and men from Roger's old regiment besides various Tichborne tenants and friends of the family. On the other hand, there were only seventeen witnesses arraigned against him; and, in his own opinion, it was his own evidence that lost him the case. He would have won, he said, "if only he could have kept his mouth shut."

The trial of this action lasted 102 days. Sergeant Ballantine led for the Claimant; and Sir John Coleridge (afterwards Lord Chief-justice), and Mr. Hawkins, Q. C. (afterwards Lord Brampton), for the trustees of the estates of Tichborne. The cross-examination of the Claimant at the hands of Sir John Coleridge lasted twenty-two days, during which the colossal ignorance he displayed was only equalled by his boldness, dexterity and the bull-dog tenacity with which he faced the ordeal. To quote Sir John's own words: "The first sixteen years of his life he has absolutely forgotten; the few facts he had told the jury were already proved, or would hereafter be shown, to be absolutely false and fabricated. Of his college life he could recollect nothing. About his amusements, his books, his music, his games, he could tell nothing. Not a word of his family, of the people with whom he lived, their habits, their persons, their very names. He had forgotten his mother's maiden name; he was ignorant of all particulars of the family estate; he remembered nothing of Stonyhurst; and in military matters he was equally deficient. Roger, born and educated in France, spoke and wrote French like a native and his favourite reading was French literature; but the Claimant knew nothing of

French. Of the 'sealed' packet he knew nothing and, when pressed, his interpretation of its contents contained the foulest and blackest calumny of the cousin whom Roger had so fondly loved. This was proved by Mr. Gosford, to whom the packet had been originally entrusted, and by the production of the duplicate which Roger had given to Miss Doughty herself. The physical discrepancy, too, was no less remarkable; for, while Roger, who took after his mother was slight and delicate, with narrow sloping shoulders, a long narrow face and thin straight dark hair, the Claimant was of enormous bulk, scaling over twenty-four stone, big-framed and burly, with a large round face and an abundance of fair and rather wavy hair. And yet, curiously enough, the Claimant undoubtedly possessed a strong likeness to several male members of the Tichborne family."

When questioned as to the impressive episode of Roger's love for his cousin, the Claimant showed himself hopelessly at sea. His answers were confused and irreconcilable. Not only could he give no precise dates, but even the broad outline of the story was beyond him. Yet, for good reasons, the Solicitor-General persisted in pressing him as to the contents of the sealed packet and compelled him to repeat the slanderous version of the incident which he had long ago given when interrogated on the point. Mrs. Radcliffe (she was not then Lady) sat in court beside her husband, and thus had the satisfaction of seeing the infamous charges brought against the fair fame of her girlhood recoil on the head of the wretch who had resorted to such villainous devices. Unfortunately, some years after Roger's disappearance, Mr. Gosford, feeling that he was neither justified in keeping the precious packet, nor in handing it to any other person, had burnt it; but, fortunately his testimony as to its contents was proved in the most complete manner by the production of the duplicate which poor Roger had given to his cousin on his last visit to Tichborne.

Where the case broke down most completely was in the matter of tattoo marks. Roger had been freely tattooed. Among other marks he bore, on his left arm, a cross, an anchor, and a heart which was testified to by the persons who had pricked them in. Orton, too, it was found out, had also been tattooed on his left arm with his initials, "A. O.," and, though neither remained, there was a mark which was sworn to be the obliteration of those letters. Small wonder then that, on the top of this damning piece of evidence, the jury declared they required to hear nothing further, upon which the Claimant's counsel, to avoid the inevitable verdict for their opponents, elected to be nonsuited. But these tactics did not save their client, for he was at once arrested, on the judge's warrant, on the charge of wilful and corrupt perjury, and committed to

Newgate where he remained until bail for £10,000 was forthcoming.

A year later, on April 23, 1873, the Claimant was arraigned before a special jury in the Court of Queen's Bench. The proceedings were of a most prolix and unusual character. Practically the same ground was covered as in the civil trial, only the process was reversed: the Claimant having now to defend instead of to attack. Many of the better-class witnesses, including the majority of Roger's brother-officers, now forsook the Claimant. There was a deal of cross-swearing. The climax of the long trial was the production by the defence of a witness to support the Claimant's account of his wreck and rescue. This was a man who called himself Jean Luie and claimed to be a Danish seaman. With a wealth of picturesque detail he told how he was one of the crew of the *Osprey* which had picked up a boat of the shipwrecked *Bella*, in which was the claimant and some of the crew, and how when the *Osprey* arrived at Melbourne, in the height of the gold fever, every man of the crew from the captain downwards had deserted the ship and gone up country. According to his story from that time forth he had seen nothing of any of the castaways; but having come to England in search of his wife he had heard of the trial. When Luie was first brought into the presence of the Claimant that astute person immediately claimed him with the greeting in Spanish *"Como esta, Luie?"*—"How are you, Luie?" The sailor with equal readiness recognised Orton as the man he had helped to rescue years before. All this sounded very convincing; but it would not stand investigation. From the beginning to end the thing was an invention; an examination of shipping records failed to find the *Osprey* so that she must have escaped the notice of the authorities in every port she had entered from the day she was launched! Of "Sailor" Luie, however, a very complete record was established. Not only were the police able to prove that, at the time he swore he was a seaman on board the *Osprey*, he was actually employed by a firm at Hull; that he had never been a seaman at all; but that he was a well-known habitual criminal and convict only recently released on a ticket-of-leave. This made things very awkward for the defence who made every effort to shake free from the taint of such perjured evidence. Dr. Kenealy, seeing his dilemma, contended that it had been concocted by Luie himself. But the damning and unanswerable fact remained—that, by his recognition of the man, the Claimant had acknowledged a previous acquaintance with him which he could only have had by being privy to the fraud.

On February 28, 1874, the one hundred and eighty-eighth day of the trial, the jury after half-an-hour's deliberation returned their verdict. They found that the defendant was not Roger

Charles Tichborne; that he was Arthur Orton; and finally that the charges made against Miss Catherine Doughty were not supported by the slightest evidence. Orton was sentenced to fourteen years' penal servitude which, assuredly, was none too heavy for offences so enormous. The trial was remarkable, not only for its inordinate length, but also for the extraordinary scenes by which it was characterised and for which Dr. Kenealy, leading counsel for the defence, was primarily responsible. His conduct was sternly denounced by the Lord Chief Justice in his summing up as: "the torrent of undisguised and unlimited abuse in which the learned counsel for the defence has thought fit to indulge," and he declared that "there never was in the history of jurisprudence a case in which such an amount of imputation and invective had been used before." After the trial was over, Dr. Kenealy tried to turn the case into a national question through the medium of a virulent paper he started with the title of the *Englishman;* and undeterred by being disbarred for his flagrant breaches of professional etiquette, he went about the country delivering the most extravagant speeches concerning the trial. He was elected Member of Parliament for Stoke, and, on April 23, 1875, moved for a royal commission of inquiry into the conduct of the Tichborne Case; but his motion was defeated by 433 votes to 1.

The verdict and sentence created enormous excitement throughout the country, for all classes, more or less, had subscribed to the defence fund. But, by the time Orton was released, in 1884, practically all interest had died away, and his effort to resuscitate it was a miserable failure. In the sworn confession which he published in the *People,* in 1895, he told the whole story of the fraud from its inception to its final denouement. Orton survived his release from prison for fourteen years, but gradually sinking into poverty, he died in obscure lodgings in Shouldham Street, Marylebone, on April 1, 1898. To the end he was a fraud and impostor for, before his death, he is said to have recanted his sworn confession, which nevertheless bore the stamp of truth and was in perfect accord with the information obtained by the prosecution, while his coffin bore the lying inscription: "Sir Roger Charles Doughty Tichborne; born 5th January, 1829; died 1st April, 1898."

VII. WOMEN AS MEN

A. THE MOTIVE FOR DISGUISE

ONE of the commonest forms of imposture—so common that it seems rooted in a phase of human nature—is that of women who disguise themselves as men. It is not to be wondered at that such attempts are made; or that they were made more often formerly when social advancement had not enlarged the scope of work available for women. The legal and economic disabilities of the gentler sex stood then so fixedly in the way of working opportunity that women desirous of making an honest livelihood took desperate chances to achieve their object. We have read of very many cases in the past; and even now the hum-drum of life is broken by the fact or the echo of some startling revelation of the kind. Only very lately the death of a person who had for many years occupied a worthy though humble position in London caused a post-mortem sensation by the discovery that the deceased individual, though looked on for about a quarter of a century as a man, a widower, and the father of a grown-up daughter, was in reality a woman. She was actually buried under the name of the man she had professed to be, Harry Lloyd.

It is not to be wondered at that in more strenuous times, when the spirit of adventure was less curbed, and initial difficulties were less deadened by convention, cases of concealment of sex were far more numerous and more easily prolonged. In an age of foreign wars, many existing barriers against success in this respect were removed by general laxity of social conditions. Perhaps I may be allowed to say at the outset that, for my own part, my mind refuses absolutely to accept that which is generally alleged in each case, that the male comrades of women concealing their proper sex were, all through, ignorant of the true facts. Human nature is opposed to such a supposition, and experience bears out the shrewdness of nature. On occasions, or even for a time, it is possible to make such successful concealments. But when we are told that a woman has gone through a whole campaign or a prolonged voyage in all the overcrowded intimacy of tent and bivouac or of cabin and forecastle, without such a secret being suspected or discovered, the narrator makes an overlarge draft on human credulity. That such comrades, and many of them, forbore to give away the secret, no matter how it had come into their possession, we may well believe. Comradeship is a strong factor in such matters, and it has its own loyalty, which is never stronger than when the various persons interested are held together by the knowledge of a common danger. But even to this there is a contra; the whole spirit of romance, even when it binds man to woman and woman to man, stands side by side with love, affection, passion—call it what you will—which opportunity can fan into flame. Never more so than in the strenuous days of fighting, when day and night are full of varying fears—when the mad turmoil of working hours and loneliness of the night forge new fetters for the binding together of the sexes.

In real life, when a man or a woman tries to escape from capture or the fear of it in the guise of the opposite sex, it is a never-ending struggle to sustain the rôle successfully. If this is so, when the whole of the energies of mind and body are devoted in singleness of purpose to the task, how then can the imposture be successfully prolonged when the mind is eternally occupied with the pressing things of the passing moments? There must infallibly be moments of self-betrayal; and there is sufficient curiosity in the average person to insure that the opportunities of such moments are not lost. Be this as it may, we must in the first instance stick to matters of fact; the record is our sheet-anchor. After all, when we learn of a case where an imposture of the kind has been successfully carried out, it is time enough to argue with convincing perspicacity that it should not have been possible.

As to record, there are quite sufficient cases to convince any reader as to the fact that, allowing for all possible error and wastage, there have been a sufficient number undetected at the time of their happening, and only made known by after-confession and by the force of ulterior circumstances. Whatever opinion we may form of the women who carried out the venture, there is neither occasion nor need to doubt the fact they were so carried out. The consideration of a few cases culled from the records of this class of successful imposture will make this plain. It would be useless, if not impossible, to make full lists of the names of women who have passed themselves off as men in the fighting world—soldiers and sailors, with side interests such as piracy, duelling, highway robbery, etc. Amongst the female soldiers are the names of Christian Davis (known as Mother Ross), Hannah Snell, Phœbe Hessel. Amongst the sailors those of Mary Talbot, Ann Mills, Hannah Whitney, Charles Waddell. In the ranks of the pirates are Mary Reid and Ann Bonney. In many of these cases are underlying romances, as of women making search for lost or absconding husbands, or of lovers making endeavours to regain the lost paradise of life together.

If there were nothing else in these little histories, their perusal in detail would well repay attention as affording proof of the boundless devotion of woman's love. No matter how badly the man may have treated the woman, no matter how heartlessly or badly he may have behaved towards her, her affection was proof against all. Indeed it makes one believe that there is some subtle self-sustaining, self-ennobling quality in womanhood which her initial self-surrender makes a constant force towards good. Even a nature which took new strength from the turmoil of battle, from the harrowing suspense of perpetual vigil, from the strain of physical weakness bravely borne, from pain and want and hunger, instead of hardening into obstinate indifference, seems to have softened as to sentiment, and been made gentle as to memory, as though the sense of wrong had been purged by the forces of affliction. All this, though the stress of campaigning may have blunted some of the conventional susceptibility of womanhood. For the after life of some of these warlike heroines showed that they had lost none of the love of admiration which marks their sex, none of their satisfaction in posing as characters other than their own. Several of them found pleasure in a new excitement different from that of battle, in the art of the stage. Whenever any of them made any effort to settle down in life after their excitement in the life of the camp or the sea, such did so at some place, and in some way congenial to herself and consistent with the life which she was leaving.

B. HANNAH SNELL.

Hannah Snell is a good instance of how the life of a woman who was not by nature averse from adventure was moulded by chance in the direction which suited her individuality. Of course, liking for a militant life, whether in conventional or exceptional form, presupposes a natural boldness of spirit, resolution, and physical hardihood—all of which this woman possessed in an eminent degree.

She was born at Worcester in 1723, one of the family of a hosier who had three sons and six daughters. In 1740, when her father and mother were dead, she went to live at Wapping with a sister who had married a ship carpenter named Gray. There she married a Dutch sailor, who before her baby was born, had squandered such little property as her father had left her, and then deserted her. She went back to her sister, in whose house the baby died. In 1743, she made up her mind to search for her husband. To this end she put on man's clothes and a man's name (that of her brother-in-law) and enlisted in General Guise's regiment. At Carlisle, whither the regiment was sent she learned something of a soldier's duties. In doing so she was selected by her sergeant, a man called Davis, to help him in carrying out a criminal love affair. In order to be able to warn the girl she pretended acquiescence. In revenge the sergeant reported her for an alleged neglect of some duty for which according to the barbarous system of the time she was sentenced to 600 lashes; of these she had actually received 500 when on the intervention of some of the officers the remaining hundred were foregone. After this, fearing further aggression on the part of the revengeful petty officer she deserted. She walked all the way to Portsmouth—a journey which occupied a whole month—where she again enlisted as a marine in Fraser's regiment, which was shortly ordered on foreign service to the East Indies. There was a storm on the way out, during which she worked manfully at the pumps. When the ship had passed Gibraltar there was another bad storm in which she was wrecked. Hannah Snell found her way to Madeira and thence to the Cape of Good Hope. Her ship joined in the taking of Arcacopong on the Coromandel Coast; in which action Hannah fought so bravely that she was praised by her officers. Later on she assisted in the siege of Pondicherry which lasted nearly three months before it had to be abandoned. In the final attempt she served on picket duty and had to ford, under fire, a river breast high. During the struggle she received six bullets in the right leg, five in the left leg, and one in the abdomen. Her fear was not of death but discovery of her sex through the last-named wound. By the friendly aid of a black woman, however, she avoided this danger. She managed to extract the bullet herself, with her finger and thumb, and the wound made a good cure. This wound caused her a delay of some weeks during which her ship had to leave for Bombay and was delayed five weeks by a leak. Poor Hannah was again unfortunate in her officers;

one of them to whom she had refused to sing had her put in irons and given a dozen lashes. In 1749 she went to Lisbon, where she learned by chance that her husband had met at Genoa the death penalty by drowning, for a murder which he had committed. Discovery of her sex and her identity would have been doubly dangerous now; but happily she was able to conceal her alarm and so escaped detection. She got back to London through Spithead and once more found shelter in the house of her sister who at once recognised her in spite of her disguise. Her fine singing voice, which had already caused her to be flogged, now stood her in good stead. She applied for and obtained an engagement at the Royalty theatre, Wellclose square; and appeared with success as *Bill Bobstay* a sailor and *Fireloch* a soldier. She remained on the stage for some months, always wearing male dress. The government of the day gave her, on account of the hardships she had endured, a pension of £20 per annum. Later on she took a public-house at Wapping. The sign of her hostelry became noted. On one side of it was painted in effigy *The British Tar* and on the other *The Valiant Marine,* and underneath *The Widow in masquerade,* or the *Female Warrior.*

As Hannah appeared during her adventurous career as both soldier and sailor she affords, in herself, an illustrious example of female courage as well as female duplicity in both of the services.

C. LA MAUPIN.

The majority of the readers of the English-speaking race who enjoy Théophile Gautier's fascinating romance *Mademoiselle de Maupin* are not aware that the heroine was a real person. The novelist has of course made such alterations as are required to translate crude fact into more elegant fiction, and to obliterate so far as can be done the criminal or partly-criminal aspect of the lady's venturous career. But such is one of the chief duties of an artist in fiction. Though he may be an historian, in a sense, he is not limited to the occasional bareness of truth. His object is not that his work shall be true but rather what the French call *vraisemblable.* In narrative, as in most arts, crudeness is rather a fault than a virtue, so that the writer who looks for excellence in his work has without losing force, to fill up the blanks left by the necessary excision of fact by subtleties of thought and graces of description, so that the fulness or rotundity of the natural curves shall always be maintained. In truth the story of *La Maupin* is so laden with passages of excitement and interest that any writer on the subject has only to make an agreeable choice of episodes sufficiently dramatic, and consistent with each other, to form a cohesive narrative. Such a work has in it possibilities of great success—if only the author has the genius of a Théophile Gautier to set it forth. The real difficulty which such an one would have to contend against would be to remove the sordidness, the reckless passion, the unscrupulousness, the criminal intent which lies behind such a character.

The Mademoiselle de Maupin of real life was a singer at the Opera in Paris at the end of the seventeenth century. She was the daughter of a man of somewhat humble extraction engaged in secretarial work with the Count d'Armagnac; and whilst only a girl married a man named Maupin employed in the province. With him she had lived only a few months when she ran away with a maitre d'armes *(anglicè,* a fencing master) named Serane. If this individual had no other good quality in matters human or divine, he was at least a good teacher of the sword. His professional arts were used in the service of his inamorata, who became herself an excellent swordsman even in an age when swordsmanship had an important place in social life. It may have been the sexual equality implied by the name which gave the young woman the idea, but thenceforth she became a man in appearance;—in reality, in so far as such a metamorphosis can be accomplished by courage, recklessness, hardihood, unscrupulousness, and a willing obedience to all the ideas which passion and sensuality can originate and a greed of notoriety carry into execution.

In a professional tour from Paris to Marseilles, in which she as an actress took the part of a man, she gained the affections of the flighty daughter of a rich merchant of Marseilles; and, as a man, ran away with her. Being pursued, they sought refuge in a convent—a place which at that age it was manifestly easier to get into than to get out of. Here the two remained for a few days, during which, by the aid of histrionic and other arts, the actress obviated the necessary suspicions of her foolish companion and kept danger away. All the while La Maupin was conscious that an irate and rich father was in hot search for his missing daughter, and she knew that any talk about the venture would infallibly lose her the girl's fortune, besides getting herself within the grip of the law. So she decided on a bold scheme of escape from the convent, whereby she might obliterate her tracks. A nun of the convent had died and her body was awaiting burial. In the night La Maupin exchanged the body of the dead nun for the living one of her own victim. Having thus got her companion out of the convent, she set the building on fire to cover up everything, and escaped in secret to a neighbouring village, taking with her by force the girl, who naturally enough was disillusioned and began to have scruples as to the wisdom of her conduct. In the village they remained hidden for a few weeks, during which time the repentance of the poor girl became a fixed quantity. An attempt, well supported, was made to arrest the ostensible man; but this was foiled by the female swordsman who killed one of the would-be captors and dangerously wounded two others. The girl, however, made good her escape; secretly she fled from her deceiver and reached her parents in safety. But the hue and cry was out after La Maupin, whose identity was now known. She was pursued, captured, and placed in gaol to await trial. The law was strong and inexorable; the erring woman who had thus outraged so many conventions was condemned to be burned alive.

But abstract law and the executive are quite different things—at least they were in France at the close of the seventeenth century: as indeed they are occasionally in other countries and at varying times. La Maupin, being a woman and a clever one, procured sufficient influence to have the execution postponed, and so had the full punishment delayed, if not entirely avoided. More than this, she managed to get back to Paris and so to begin her noxious career all over again. Of course she had strong help from her popularity. She was a favourite at the opera, and the class which patronises and supports this kind of artistic effort is a rich and powerful one, which governments do not care to displease by the refusal of such a small favour as making the law hold its hand with regard to an erring favourite.

But La Maupin's truculent tendencies were not to be restrained. In Paris in 1695 whilst she was one of the audience at a theatre she took umbrage at some act or speech of one of the comedians playing in the piece, and leaving her seat went round to the stage and caned him in the presence of the audience. The actor, M. Dumenil, an accomplished and favourite performer but a man of peaceful disposition, submitted to the affront and took no action in the matter. La Maupin, however, suffered, through herself, the penalty of her conduct. She had entered on a course of violence which became a habit. For some years she flourished and exercised all the tyrannies of her own sex and in addition those habitual to men which came from expert use of the sword. Thus she went attired as a man to a ball given by a Prince of the blood. In that garb she treated a fellow-guest, a woman, with indecency; and she was challenged by three different men—each of whom, when the consequent fight came on, she ran through the body, after which she returned to the ball. Shortly afterwards she fought and wounded a man, M. de Servan, who had affronted a woman. For these escapades she was again pardoned. She then went to Brussels where she lived under the protection of Count Albert of Bavaria, the Elector. With him she remained until the quarrel, inevitable in such a life, came. After much bickering he agreed to her demand of a settlement, but in order to show his anger by affronting her he sent the large amount of his involuntary bequest by the servile hand of the husband of his mistress, Countess d'Arcos, who had supplanted her, with a curt message that she must leave Brussels at once. The bearer of such a message to such a woman as La Maupin had probably reckoned on an unfriendly reception; but he evidently underestimated her anger. Not contented with flinging at his head the large *douceur* of which he was the bearer, she expressed in her direct way her unfavourable opinion, of him, of his master, and of the message which he had carried for the latter. She ended her tirade by kicking him downstairs, with the justification for her form of physical violence that she would not sully her sword with his blood.

From Brussels she went to Spain as *femme de chambre* to the Countess Marino but returned to Paris in 1704. Once more she took up her work as an opera singer; or rather she tried to take it up, but she had lost her vogue, and the public would have none of her. As a matter of fact, she was only just above thirty years of age, which should under normal circumstances be the beginning of a woman's prime. But the life she had been leading since her early girlhood was not one which made for true happiness or for physical health; she was prematurely old, and her artistic powers were worn out.

Still, her pluck, and the obstinacy on which it was grafted, remained. For a whole year she maintained a never-failing struggle for her old supremacy, but without avail. Seeing that all was lost, she left the stage and returned to her husband who, realising that she was rich, managed to reconcile whatever shreds of honour he had to her infamous record. The Church, too, accepted her—and her riches—within its sheltering portals. By the aid of a tolerant priest she got absolution, and two years after her retirement from the opera she died in a convent in all the odour of sanctity.

D. MARY EAST

The story of Mary East is a pitiful one, and gives a picture of the civil life of the eighteenth century which cannot be lightly forgotten. The condition of things has so changed that already we almost need a new terminology in order that we may understand as our great-grandfathers did. Take for instance the following sentence and try individually how many points in it there are, the full meaning of which we are unable to understand:

"A young fellow courted one Mary East, and for him she conceived the greatest liking; but he going upon the highway, was tried for a robbery and cast, but was afterwards transported."

The above was written by an accomplished scholar, a Doctor of Divinity, rector of an English parish. At the time of its writing, 1825, every word of it was entirely comprehensible. If a reader of that time could see it translated into modern phraseology he would be almost as much surprised as we are when we look back upon an age holding possibilities no longer imaginable.

"Going upon the highway" was in Mary East's time and a hundred years later a euphemism for becoming a highway robber; "cast" meant condemned to death; "transported" meant exiled to a far distant place where one was guarded, and escape from which was punishable with death. Moreover robbery was at this time a capital offence.

In 1736, when Mary East was sixteen, life was especially hard on women. Few honest occupations were open to them, and they were subject to all the hardships consequent on a system in which physical weakness was handicapped to a frightful extent. When this poor girl was bereft of her natural hope of a settlement in life she determined, as the least unattractive form of living open to her, to remain single. About the same time a friend of hers arrived at the same resolution but by a different road, her course being guided thereto by having "met with many crosses in love." The two girls determined to join forces; and on consulting as to ways and means decided that the likeliest way to avoid suspicion was to live together under the guise of man and wife. The toss of a coin decided their respective rôles, the "breeches part" as it is called in the argot of the theatre, falling to East.

The combined resources of the girls totalled some thirty pounds sterling, so after buying masculine garb for Mary they set out to find a place where they were unknown and so might settle down in peace. They found the sort of place they sought in the neighbourhood of Epping Forest where, there being a little public-house vacant, Mary—now under the name of James How—became the tenant. For some time they lived in peace at Epping, with the exception of a quarrel forced by a young gentleman on the alleged James How in which the latter was wounded in the hand. It must have been a very one-sided affair, for when the injured "man" took action he was awarded £500 damages—a large sum in those days and for such a cause. With this increase to their capital the two women moved to Limehouse on the east side of London where they took at Limehouse-hole a more important public-house. This they managed in so excellent a manner that they won the respect of their neighbours and throve exceedingly.

After a time they moved from Limehouse to Poplar where they bought another house and added to their little estate by the purchase of other houses.

Peace, hard work, and prosperity marked their life thence-forward, till fourteen years had passed since the beginning of their joint venture.

Peace and prosperity are, however, but feeble guardians to weakness. Nay, rather are they incentive to evil doing. For all these years the two young women had conducted themselves with such rectitude, and observed so much discretion, that even envy could not assail them through the web of good repute which they had woven round their masquerade. Alone they lived, keeping neither female servant nor male assistant. They were scrupulously honest in their many commercial dealings and, absolutely punctual in their agreements and obligations. James How took a part in the public life of his locality, filling in turn every parish office except those of Constable and Churchwarden. From the former he was excused on account of the injury to his hand from which he had never completely recovered. Regarding the other his time had not yet come, but he was named for Churchwarden in the year following to that in which a bolt fell from the blue, 1730. It came in this wise: A woman whose name of coverture was Bently, and who was now resident in Poplar, had known the alleged James How in the days when they were both young. Her own present circumstances were poor and she looked on the prosperity of her old acquaintance as a means to her own betterment. It was but another instance of the old crime of "blackmail." She sent to the former Mary East for a loan of £10, intimating that if the latter did not send it she would make known the secret of her sex. The poor panic-stricken woman foolishly complied with the demand, thus forcing herself deeper into the mire of the other woman's unscrupulousness. The forced loan, together with Bently's fears for her own misdeed procured immunity for some fifteen years from further aggression. At the end of that time, however, under the renewed pressure of need Bently repeated her demand. "James How" had not the sum by her, but she sent £5—another link in the chain of her thraldom.

From that time on there was no more peace for poor Mary East. Her companion of nearly thirty-five years died and she, having a secret to guard and no assistance being possible, was more helpless than ever and more than ever under the merciless yoke of the blackmailer. Mrs. Bently had a fair idea of how to play her own despicable game. As her victim's fear was her own stock-in-trade she supplemented the sense of fear which she knew to exist by a conspiracy strengthened by all sorts of schemes to support its seeming *bona fides*. She took in two male accomplices and, thus enforced, began operations. Her confederates called on James How, one armed with a constable's staff, the other appearing as one of the "thief-takers" of the gang of the notorious magistrate, Fielding—an evil product of an evil time. Having confronted How they told him that they had come by order of Mr. Justice Fielding to arrest him for the commission of a robbery over forty years before, alleging that they were aware of his being a woman. Mary East, though quite innocent of any such offence but acutely conscious of her imposture of manhood, in her dismay sought the aid of a friend called Williams who understood and helped her. He went to the magistrates of the district and then to Sir John Fielding to make inquiries and claim protection. During his absence the two villains took Mary East from her house and by threats secured from her a draft on Williams for £100. With this in hand they released their victim who was even more anxious than themselves not to let the matter have greater publicity than it had already obtained. However, Justice demanded a further investigation, and one of the men being captured—the other had escaped—was tried, and being found guilty, was sentenced to imprisonment for four years together with four appearances in the pillory.

Altogether Mary East and her companion had lived together as husband and wife for nearly thirty-five years, during which time they had honestly earned, and by self-denial saved, over four thousand pounds sterling and won the good opinion of all with whom they had come in contact. They were never known to cook a joint of meat for their own use, to employ any help, or to entertain private friends in their house. They were cautious, careful, and discreet in every way and seemed to live their lives in exceeding blamelessness.

VIII. HOAXES, ETC.

THERE is a class of imposture which must be kept apart from others of its kind, or at least ear-marked in such wise that there can be no confusion of ideas regarding it. This includes all sorts of acts which, though often attended with something of the same result as other efforts to mislead, are yet distinguished from them by intention. They have—whatever may be their results—a jocular and humorous intention. Such performances are called hoaxes. These, though amusing to their perpetrators and to certain sportive persons, and though generally causing a due amount of pain and loss to those on whom they are inflicted, usually escape the condign and swift punishment which they deserve. It is generally held that humour, like charity, covereth a multitude of sins. So be it. We are all grateful for a laugh no matter who may suffer.

A. TWO LONDON HOAXES

Not many years ago, in one of the popular dairy-refreshment shops in Holborn, the prim manageress and her white-capped waitresses were just commencing their day's work when a couple of sturdy green-aproned men swooped down on the place from a large pantechnicon van, and to the amazement of the young ladies commenced to clear the shop.

"There you are Bill. Hand up them chairs, and look slippy."

"Right o', mate."

"Good gracious me, what are you men doing?" shrieked the alarmed manageress.

"Doing, miss, doing? Why moving the furniture. This is the lot ain't it?"

"No, no, no; there must be some mistake. You must have come to the wrong place."

"Mistake, wrong place? No miss. 'Ere, look where's that letter?" And Jack placed a begrimed document before the lady.

The letter seemed right enough. It read beautifully, a plain direction to clear the shop and remove the stuff elsewhere; it only lacked the official heading of the company. But the joint inspection was rudely broken in upon by the arrival of a couple of the knights of the brush who had come "to do the chimbley, maam"; and ere they could be disposed of vans of coals began to draw up, more pantechnicons, more sweeps, loads of furniture, butchers with prime joints, plump birds from the poulterers, fish of every conceivable kind, noisy green-grocer boys, staggering under huge loads of vegetables; florists "to decorate," gasfitters, carpenters "to take down the counter, miss"; others "to put it up."

Pandemonium is quiet compared with that shop. The poor manageress was in tears, deafened with the exasperated, swearing representatives of, apparently, all the tradesmen for miles around. The thing had been well done. No sooner had the provision merchants worked clear and the streams of vans, waggons and carts been backed away to the accompaniment of much lurid language, than ladies began to arrive with boxes of mysterious long garments which, they assured the indignant lady in charge, they were instructed were urgently needed for an event they referred to as "interesting." There was no monotony, for fast and furious—very furious sometimes—came other maidens laden with more boxes and still more boxes, filled with costumes, bonnets, and other creations dear to the feminine mind. Then came servants "in answer to your advertisement, madam." They flocked in from all directions, north, south, east and west. Never was seen such a concourse of servants: dignified housekeepers, housemaids, parlourmaids, and every other sort of maid, seemed to be making for that unfortunate manageress. Sleek-looking butlers popped in, as uniformed nurses popped out. Window-cleaners had to be torn from the windows they insisted they had got orders to clean; carpet beaters sought carpets which did not exist. Never had mortal—aye and immortal—requirements been thought out with more thoughtful care. From the needs of the unborn baby, to the "poor departed one," whom melancholy gentlemen in seedy black came to measure, all were remembered, and the man for whose especial benefit presumably were intended beautiful wreaths, crosses, harps, etc., which kept constantly arriving. Throughout that live-long day to the "dewy eve" beloved of the poet the game went merrily on.

As a hoax the thing was worked for all it was worth. Not only had shoals of letters evidently been sent out, but advertisements, too, had been freely distributed among the press. Needless to say that, despite the closest investigations, its author or authors, discreetly silent, remained unknown.

The joke was not new by any means. Well nigh a century before mischief-loving Theodore Hook had stirred all London by a similar prank—the famous Berners Street Hoax. In those days Berners Street was a quiet thoroughfare inhabited by fairly well-to-do families. Indeed it was this very sedate quietness which drew upon it Hook's unwelcome attention. Fixing on one of the houses, which happened to be adorned with a brass plate, he made a wager with a brother wag that he would cause that particular house to become the talk of the town: and he certainly did—for not only the town, but all England shrieked with laughter when the result of his little manœuvre became known.

One morning, soon after breakfast, waggons laden with coals began to draw up before the house with the brass plate, No. 54. These were quickly succeeded with tradespeople by the dozen with various commodities. These in turn were followed by van loads of furniture; followed by a hearse with a coffin and a number of mourning coaches. Soon the street became choked: for, what with the goods dumped down as near as possible to the house—pianos, organs, and cart loads of furniture of all descriptions, the anxious tradesmen, and the laughing mob of people quickly attracted to the scene, confusion reigned supreme. About this time the Lord Mayor and other notabilities began to arrive in their carriages. His Lordship's stay was short. He was driven to Marlborough Street police office where he informed the magistrate that he had received a note purporting to come from Mrs. T., the victimised widow resident at No. 54, saying she was confined to her room and begging his lordship to do her the favour of calling on her on important business. Meanwhile, the trouble in Berners Street was growing serious, and officers belonging to the Marlborough Street office were at once sent to keep order. For a time even they were helpless. Never was such a strange meeting: barbers with wigs; mantlemakers with band-boxes; opticians with their various articles of trade. Presently there arrived a couple of fashionable physicians, an accoucheur, and a dentist. There were clockmakers, carpet manufacturers and wine merchants, all loaded with specimens of their trade; brewers with barrels of ale, curiosity dealers with sundry knick-knacks; cartloads of potatoes; books, prints, jewellery, feathers and furbelows of all kinds; ices and jellies; conjuring tricks; never was such a conglomeration. Then, about five o'clock servants of all kinds began to troop in to apply for situations. For a time the police officers were powerless. Vehicles were jammed and interlocked; the exasperated drivers were swearing, and the disappointed tradesmen were maddened by the malicious fun of the crowd who were enjoying the joke. Some of the vans were overturned and many of the tradesmens' goods came to grief; while some of the casks of ale became the prey of the delighted spectators. All through the day and late into the night this extraordinary state of things continued, to the dismay and terror of the poor lady and the other inmates of the house with the brass plate.

Theodore Hook had taken precautions to secure a good seat for the performance, having taken furnished-apartments just opposite the house of his victim, where he posted himself with one or two companions to enjoy the scene. Hook's connection with the mad joke was, fortunately for him, not known until long afterwards; it seems he had devoted three or four whole days to writing the letters, all couched in ladylike style. In the end the novelist seems to have been rather frightened at the result of his little joke, for he made a speedy departure to the country; and there is no doubt that, had he been publicly known as its author, he would have fared badly.

B. THE CAT HOAX

One very amusing variation of the countless imitations, which the success of this trick gave rise to, was the "cat hoax" at Chester, in August, 1815. It was at the time when it had been determined to send Napoleon to St. Helena. One morning, a number of hand bills were distributed in and around Chester, stating that, owing to the island of St. Helena being invested with rats, the government required a number of cats for deportation. Sixteen shillings were offered for "every athletic full-grown tom cat, ten shillings for every adult female puss, and a half-crown for every thriving kitten that could swill milk, pursue a ball of thrĕad, or fasten its young fangs in a dying mouse." An address was given at which the cats were to be delivered; but it proved to be an empty house. The advertisement resulted in the victimisation of hundreds of people. Men, women, and children streamed into the city from miles around laden with cats of every description. Some hundreds were brought in, and the scene before the door of the empty house is said to have baffled description. When the hoax was discovered many of the cats were liberated; the following morning no less than five hundred dead cats were counted floating down the river Dee.

C. THE MILITARY REVIEW

Practical jokes of this nature have more than once led to serious results. In the summer of 1812 a report was extensively circulated that a grand military review was to be held on the 19th of June. Booths were erected and as many as twenty thousand people assembled, despite the efforts of the authorities who, when they learned what was happening, posted men in the several roads leading to the heath to warn the people that they had been hoaxed. But their efforts were useless. The rumour was believed and the contradiction ignored; vehicles, horsemen and pedestrians pushed on to their destination. When, however, the day wore on without any appearance of the promised military pageant, the crowd grew angry and then broke out in acts of violence. The heath was set on fire. Messengers were sent off express to London, and a detachment of the guards had to be marched down to quell the mob. In the disorder one poor woman was thrown out of a chaise and picked up in an unconscious condition.

D. THE TOLL-GATE

Many distinguished actors have been very fond of playing practical jokes and perpetrating hoaxes. Young, the tragedian, was one day driving in a gig with a friend on the outskirts of London. Pulling up at a turn-pike gate he noticed the name of the toll-collector written up over the door. Calling to him the woman, the wife of that functionary, who appeared to be in charge of the gate, he politely told her that he particularly wished to see Mr. ——, naming the toll-collector, on a matter of importance. Impressed by Young's manner, she promptly sent for her husband, who was working in a neighbouring field. Hastily washing himself and putting on a clean coat he presented himself. The actor gravely said: "I paid for a ticket at the last gate, and was told that it would free me through this one. As I wish to be scrupulously exact, will you kindly tell me whether such is the case?" "Why of course it is?" "Can I then pass through without paying?" The toll-collector's reply and his vituperation as the travellers passed on had better, perhaps, be left to the imagination.

E. THE MARRIAGE HOAX

Hoaxes are sometimes malicious, and often cruel, as the following instance will show: A young couple were about to be married in Birmingham when those officiating—it was a Jewish wedding—were startled by the delivery of a telegram from London with the message: "Stop marriage at once. His wife and children have arrived in London and will come on to Birmingham." The bride fainted and the bridegroom was frantically perturbed at thus summarily being provided with a wife and family. But it was useless; the unhappy man had to make the best of his way through an exasperated crowd full of sympathy for the wronged girl. Inquiry, however, showed her friends that the whole thing was a hoax—possibly worked by some revengeful rival of the man whose happiness had been so unexpectedly deferred.

F. BURIED TREASURE

Most people have heard of the "Spanish Treasure swindle" and, though less elaborate than the original, a variation of it practised on a French merchant was rather "cute." One morning he received an anonymous communication advising him that a box of treasure was buried in his garden the exact position of which would be pointed out to him, if he agreed to divide the spoil. He rose at once to the bait, met his generous informant, and before long the pair were merrily at work with pickaxe and shovel. Sure enough before long their exertions were awarded by the unearthing of a box full of silver coins. The hoard proved to consist of sixteen hundred five-franc pieces; and the delighted merchant, after carefully counting them out into two piles, offered one lot to his partner as his share. That worthy, after contemplating the heap for a minute or two, observed that it would be rather a heavy load to carry to the railway station, and said he would prefer, if it could be managed, to have the amount in gold or notes. "Certainly, certainly!" was the reply. The two men walked up to the house and the business was settled to their mutual satisfaction. Twenty-four hours later, the merchant took a very different view of the transaction; for examination discovered there was not one genuine five-franc piece among the whole lot.

G. DEAN SWIFT'S HOAX

One of the most beautiful hoaxes ever perpetrated was one for which Swift was responsible. He caused a broad-sheet to be printed and circulated which purported to be the "last dying speech" of one Elliston, a street robber, in which the condemned thief was made to say: "Now as I am a dying man, I have done something which may be of use to the public. I have left with an honest man—the only honest man I was ever acquainted with—the names of all my wicked brethren, the places of their abode, with a short account of the chief crimes they have committed, in many of which I have been their accomplice, and heard the rest from their own mouths. I have likewise set down names of those we call our setters, of the wicked houses we frequent, and all of those who receive and buy our stolen goods. I have solemnly charged this honest man, and have received his promise upon oath, that whenever he hears of any rogue to be tried for robbery or housebreaking, he will look into his list, and if he finds the name there of the thief concerned, to send the whole paper to the Government. Of this I here give my companions fair and public warning, and hope they will take it." So successful, we are told, was the Dean's ruse that, for many years afterwards, street robberies were almost unknown.

H. HOAXED BURGLARS

The above ingenious device recalls another occasion when some gentlemen who made burglary their profession, and who had been paying a midnight visit to the house of a Hull tradesman were sadly "sold." They found the cash-box lying handy, and, to their delight, weighty; so heavy indeed that they did not stay to help themselves to anything further. Next morning the cash-box was found not far from the shop and its contents in an ash-pit close by. After all the trouble they had taken, to say nothing of the risks they had run, the burglars found their prize consisted only of a lump of lead, and that their intended victim had been too artful for them.

I. BOGUS SAUSAGES

As an example of how a dishonest penny may be turned the following incident would be hard to beat.

Two weary porters at the King's Cross terminus of the Great Northern Railway were thinking about going home, when a breathless, simple-looking countryman rushed up to them with anxious enquiries for a certain train. It had gone. He was crushed. "Whatever was he to do? He had been sent up from Cambridge with a big hamper of those sausages for which the University town is celebrated—a very special order. Was there no other train?" "No." The poor fellow seemed overwhelmed. "As it is too late to find another market," he complained, "the whole lot will be lost." Then a happy thought seemed to strike him as more of the railway men gathered round, and he inquired ingratiatingly, "Would you care to buy the sausages; if you would, you could have them for fourpence a pound? If I keep them, they will probably go bad before I can dispose of them." The idea took—"Real Cambridge Sausages" at fourpence a pound was not to be sneezed at. The dainties, neatly packed in pounds, went like the proverbial hot cakes. Shouldering the empty basket, and bidding his customers a kindly good-night, the yokel set off to find a humble lodging for the night. Grateful smiles greeted the purchasers when they got home. Frying pans were got out and the sausages were popped in, and never was such a sizzling heard in the railway houses—or rather never should such a sizzling have been heard. But somehow they didn't sizzle. "They are uncommon dry; seem to have no fat in 'em," said the puzzled cook. They were dry, very dry, for closer investigation showed that the "prime Cambridge" were nothing but skins stuffed with dry bread! The railway staff of King's Cross were long anxious to meet that simple countryman from Cambridge.

J. THE MOON HOAX

One of the most stupendous hoaxes, and one foisted on the credulity of the public with the most complete success, was the famous Moon Hoax which was published in the pages of the New York *Sun* in 1835. It purported to be an account of the great astronomical discoveries of Sir John Herschel at the Cape of Good Hope, through the medium of a mighty telescope, a single lens of which weighed nearly seven tons. It was stated to be reproduced from the Supplement to the Edinburgh *Journal of Science,* though as a matter of fact, the *Journal* had then been defunct some years. In graphic language, and with a wealth of picturesque detail, the wonders of the Moon as revealed to the great astronomer and his assistants were set forth. A great inland sea was observed, and "fairer shores never angel coasted on a tour of pleasure." The beach was "of brilliant white sand, girt with wild castellated rocks apparently of green marble, varied at chasms, occurring every two hundred feet, with grotesque blocks of chalk or gypsum, and feathered and festooned at the summit with the clustering foliage of unknown trees." There were hills of amethysts "of a diluted claret colour"; mountains fringed with virgin gold; herds of brown quadrupeds resembling diminutive bison fitted with a sort of "hairy veil" to protect their eyes from the extremes of light and darkness; strange monsters—a combination of unicorn and goat; pelicans, cranes, strange amphibious creatures, and a remarkable biped beaver. The last was said to resemble the beaver of the earth excepting that it had no tail and walked only upon its two feet. It carried its young in its arms like a human-being, and its huts were constructed better and higher than those of many savage tribes; and, from the smoke, there was no doubt it was acquainted with the use of fire. Another remarkable animal observed, was described as having an amazingly long neck, a head like a sheep, bearing two spiral horns, a body like a deer, but with its fore-legs disproportionately long as also its tail which was very bushy and of a snowy whiteness, curling high over its rump and hanging two or three feet by its side.

But even these marvels fade into insignificance compared with the discovery of the lunarian men "four feet in height, covered, except on the face, with short and glossy copper-coloured hair, with wings composed of a thin membrane." "In general symmetry they were infinitely superior to the orang-outang"—which statement could hardly have been regarded as complimentary; and, though described as "doubtless innocent and happy creatures," the praise was rather discounted by the mention that some of their amusements would "but ill comport with our terrestrial notions of decorum." In the "Vale of the Triads," with beautiful temples built of polished sapphire, a superior race of the punariant were found, "eminently happy and even polite," eating gourds and red cucumbers; and further afield yet another race of the vespertilio-homo, or man-bat, were seen through the wonderful telescope of "infinitely greater personal beauty . . . scarcely less lovely than the general representation of angels."

Such were a few of the marvels told of in the Moon story; and, though one may laugh at them as they stand, shorn of their clever verbiage and quasi-scientific detail, at the time of publication they were seriously accepted, for the popular mind, even among the educated classes, was then imbued with the fanciful anticipators of vast lunar discoveries heralded in the astronomical writings of Thomas Dick, LL.D., of the Union College of New York. Scarcely anything could have been brought forward too extravagant for the general credulity on the subject then prevailing; and this well-timed satire, "out-heroding Herod" in its imaginative creations, supplied to satiety the morbid appetite for scientific wonders then raging. By its plausible display of scientific erudition it successfully duped, with few exceptions, the whole civilised world.

At the time, the hoax was very generally attributed to a French astronomer, M. Nicollet, a legitimist who fled to America in 1830. He was said to have written it with the twofold object of raising the wind, and of "taking in" Arago, a rival astronomer. But its real author was subsequently found to be Richard Adams Locke, who declared that his original intention was to satirise the extravagances of Dick's writings, and to make certain suggestions which he had some diffidence in putting forward seriously. Whatever may have been his object, the work, as a hit, was unrivalled. For months the press of America and Europe teemed with the subject; the account was printed and published in many languages and superbly illustrated. But, finally, Sir John Herschel's signed denial gave the mad story its quietus.

IX. THE CHEVALIER D'EON

IN all the range of doubtful personalities there is hardly any one whom convention has treated worse than it has the individual known in his time—and after—as The Chevalier d'Eon. For about a hundred and fifty years he has been written of—and spoken of for the first half century of that time—simply as a man who masqueraded in woman's clothes. There seems to be just sufficient truth in this to save certain writers on the subject from the charge of deliberate lying—a record which, even if it is to be posthumous, no man of integrity aims at; but it is abundantly evident that the rumour, which in time became a charge, was originally set on foot deliberately by his political enemies, who treated him and his memory without either consideration or even the elements of honourable truth. To begin with, here are the facts of his long life.

Charles-Genevieve — Louis-Auguste-Andre — Timothée d'Eon de Beaumont was born in 1728 in Tonnerre in Yonne, a department of France in the old province of Burgundy. His father, Louis d'Eon, was a parliamentary barrister. As a youth he was so apt in his studies at the Collège Mazarin that he received by special privilege his degree of

Doctor in Canon and Civil Law before the age appointed for the conferring of such honour, and was then enrolled in the list of parliamentary barristers in Paris. At first he had been uncertain which department of life he should undertake. He swayed on one side towards the church, on the other towards the world of letters and *beaux-arts*. He was by habit an athlete, and was so good a swordsman that later on he had no rival in fencing except the Chevalier de Saint-George. In his twenty-fifth year he published two remarkable books. One was on the political administration of ancient and modern people, and the other on Phases of Finance in France at different times. (The latter was afterwards published in German at Berlin in 1774, and so impressed the then King of Prussia that he gave orders that its ideas were to be carried into practical effect.)

In 1755 the Prince de Conti, to whose notice the Chevalier had been brought by the above books, asked the king (Louis XV) to send him to Russia on a secret mission with the Chevalier Douglas; and from that time till the king's death in 1774 he was his trusted, loyal agent and correspondent. D'Eon's special mission was to bring the courts of France and Rusisa closer than had been their wont, and also to obtain for the Prince de Conti, who was seeking the Dukedom of Finland and the Kingship of Poland, the favour of the Empress Elizabeth—a difficult task, which had already cost

THE CHEVALIER D'EON

M. de Valcroissant a spell of imprisonment. In order to accomplish his mission, d'Eon disguised himself as a woman, and in this guise he was able to creep into the good graces of the Empress. He became her "reader" and was thus enabled to prepare her for the reception of the secret purposes of his king. In the following year he returned to France whence he was immediately sent again to St. Petersburg with the title of Secretary of Embassy. But this time he went in his man's clothes and as the brother of the pretended female reader. By this time he had been made a lieutenant of dragoons. He came in spite of the Russian Chancellor Bestuchéf, who saw in the young soldier-diplomat *"un subject dangereux et capable de boulverser l'empire."* This time his real mission was to destroy in the mind of the Empress faith in Bestuchéf, who was trying to hold the Russian army inactive and so deprive France of the advantages of the Treaty of Versailles. This he did so well that he was in a position to prove to the Empress that her chancellor had betrayed her interests. Bestuchéf was arrested and his post conferred on Count Woronzow, whose attitude was altogether favourable to France. The gratitude of King Louis was shewn by his making d'Eon a captain of dragoons and conferring on him a pension of 2400 livres; he was also made censor of history and literature. D'Eon threw himself with his accustomed zeal into the service of the army and distinguished himself by his courage in the battles of Hoecht; of Ultrop, where he was wounded; of Eimbech where he put the Scotch to flight; and of Osterkirk, where at the head of 80 dragoons and 20 hussars he overthrew a battalion of the enemy.

No better conventional proof of the accepted idea of d'Eon's military worthiness can be given than the frequency and importance of the occasions on which he was honoured by the carrying of despatches. He brought news of his successful negotiations for the peace of Versailles from Vienna in 1757. He was also sent with the Ratification of the Treaty. He carried the despatches of the great victory of the troops of Maria Theresa, forestalling the Austrian courier by a day and a half, although he had a broken leg.

When next sent to Russia, d'Eon was sent as minister plenipotentiary, an office which he held up to 1762 when to the regret of the Empress he was recalled. When he was leaving, Woronzow, the successor of Bestuchéf, said to him, "I am sorry you are going, although your first journey with Chevalier Douglas cost my sovereign 250,000 men and more than 5,000,000 roubles." D'Eon answered: "Your excellency ought to be happy that your sovereign and his minister have gained more glory and reputation than any others in the world." On his return d'Eon was appointed to the regiment d'Autchamp and gazetted as adjutant to Marshal de Broglie. Then he was sent to Russia for the fourth time as minister plenipotentiary in place of Baron de Breuteuil. But Peter III was dethroned, so the out-going Ambassador remained in Russia, and d'Eon went to England as secretary to the Embassy of the Duke de Nivernais in 1762.

After the Peace of 1763 d'Eon was chosen by the King of England to carry the despatches. He received for this office the Star of St. Louis from the breast of the king, who on giving it said it was for the bravery which he had displayed as a soldier, and for the intelligence which he had shown in the negotiations between London and St. Petersburg.

At this time all went well with him. But his good fortune was changed by the bitter intrigues of his enemies. He was devoted to the king, but had, almost as a direct consequence, the enmity of the courtesans who surrounded him and wished for the opportunity of plucking him at their leisure. He had an astonishing knowledge on all matters of finance, and apprised the king privately of secret matters which his ministers tried to hide from him. The Court had wind of that direct correspondence with his majesty and therewith things were so managed that the diplomatist got into trouble. Madame de Pompadour surprised the direct correspondence between the king and d'Eon, with the result that the latter was persecuted by the jealous courtiers who intrigued, until in 1765 he was replaced at the Embassy of London by the Count de Guerchy and he himself became the mark for all sorts of vexations and persecutions. His deadly enemy, the Count de Guerchy, tried to have him poisoned, but the attempt failed. D'Eon took legal steps to punish the attempt; but every form of pressure was used to keep the case out of Court. An attempt was made to get the Attorney General to enter a *nolle prosequi;* but he refused to lend himself to the scheme, and sent the matter to the Court of King's Bench. There, despite all the difficulties of furthering such a charge against any one so protected as an ambassador, it was declared on trial that the accused was guilty of the crime charged against him. De Guerchy accordingly had to return to France; but d'Eon remained in England, though without employment. To console him King Louis gave him in 1766 a pension of 12,000 livres, and assured him that though he was ostensibly exiled this was done to cover up the protection extended to him. D'Eon, according to the report of the time, was offered a bribe of 1,200,000 livres, to give up certain state papers then in his custody; but to his honour he refused. Be the story as it may, d'Eon up to the time of the death of Louis (1774) continued to be in London the real representative of France, though without any formal appointment.

During this time one of the means employed with success by his enemies to injure the reputation of d'Eon, was to point out that he had passed himself as a woman; the disguise he wore on his first visit to Russia. His clean shaven face, his personal niceties, the correctness of his life, all came to the aid of that supposition. In England bets were made and sporting companies formed for the purpose of verifying his sex. Designs were framed for the purpose of carrying him off in order to settle the vexed question by a personal examination. Some of the efforts he had to repel by violence. In 1770 and in 1772 his friends tried to arrange that he should be allowed to return to France; but he refused all offers as the Ministers insisted on making it a condition of his return that he should wear feminine apparel. After the accession of Louis XVI he obtained leave to return, free from the embarrassing restraint hitherto demanded. As he was overwhelmed with debts he placed as a guarantee in the hands of Lord Ferrers an iron casket containing important French state papers. The minister sent Beaumarcheus to redeem them, and in 1771 the Chevalier returned to France. He presented himself at Versailles in his full uniform of a captain of dragoons. The Queen (Marie Antoinette) however, wished to see him presented in female dress; so the Minister implored him to meet her wishes. He consented; and thenceforward not only wore women's clothes but called himself "La Chevalière d'Eon." In a letter addressed by him to Madame de Staël during the French revolution he spoke of himself as "citizeness of the New

Republic of France, and of the old Republic of Literature." On 2nd September, 1777 he wrote to the Count de Maurepas, "Although I detest changes of costume, yet they are hard at work at Mademoiselle Bertin's on my future and doleful dress, which however I shall cut in pieces at the first sound of the cannon shots." As a matter of fact when war with England became imminent he demanded to be allowed to take in the army the position which he had won by bravery and as the price of honourable wounds. The only reply he got was his immurement for two months in the Castle of Dijon. In 1784 he returned to England, which he never again left. In vain he appealed to the Convention and then to the First Consul to be allowed to place his sword at the service of his country; but his prayer was not listened to. Used to the practice of the sword, his circumstances being desperate, he then found in it a source of income. He gave in public, assaults-at-arms with the Chevalier de Saint-George, one of the most notable fencers of his time. At length he was given a small pension, £40, by George III, on which he subsisted during the remainder of his life. He died 23rd May, 1810.

In very fact Chevalier d'Eon is historically a much injured man. His vocation was that of a secret-service agent of a nation surrounded with enemies, and to her advantage he used his rare powers of mind and body. He was a very gallant soldier, who won distinction in the field and was wounded several times; and in his endurance and his indifference to pain whilst carrying despatches of overwhelming importance he set an example that any soldier might follow with renown. As a statesman and diplomatist, and by the use of his faculties of inductive ratiocination, he averted great dangers from his country. If there were nothing else to his credit he might well stand forth as a diplomatist who had by his own exertions overthrown a dishonest Russian Chancellor and an unscrupulous French Ambassador. Of course, as he was an agent of secret service, he had cognisance of much political and international scheming which he had at times to frustrate at the risk of all which he held dear. But, considering the time he lived in, and the dangers which he was always in the thick of, in a survey of his life the only thing a reader can find fault with is his yielding to the base idea of the flighty-minded Marie Antoinette. What, to this irresponsible butterfly of fashion, was the honour of a brave soldier or the reputation of an acute diplomatist who had deserved well of his country. Of course to her any such foolery as that to which she condemned d'Eon was but the fancy of an idle moment. But then the fancies of queens at idle moments may be altogether destructive to someone. That they may be destructive to themselves is shown in the record of the terrible atrocities of the Revolution which followed hard on the luxurious masquerades of Trianon and Versailles. Even to the

Queen of France, the Chevalier d'Eon should have been something of a guarded, if not an honoured, person. He was altogether a "king's man." He had been for many years the trusted and loyal servant of more than one king; and from the king's immediate circle the proper consideration should have been shown.

There is something pitiful in the spectacle of this old gentleman of nearly eighty years of age, who had in his time done so much, being compelled to earn a bare livelihood by the exploitation of the most sordid page in his history—a page turned more than half a century before, and then only turned at all in response to the call of public duty.

In his retirement d'Eon showed more of his real nature than had been possible to him in the strenuous days when he had to be always vigilant and ready at an instant's notice to conceal his intentions—his very thoughts. Here he showed a sensitiveness with which even his friends did not credit him. He had been so long silent as to matters of his own concern that they had begun to think he had lost the faculty not only of making the thought known, but even of the thought itself. The following paragraph from the London *Public Advertiser* of Wednesday, 16th November, 1774, shows more of the real man than may be found in any of his business letters or diplomatic reports:—

"The Chevalier d'Eon with justice complains of our public prints; they are eternally sending him to

France while he is in body and soul fixed in this country; they have lately confined him in the Bastille, when he fled to England as a country of liberty; and they lately made a Woman of him, when not one of his enemies dared to put his manhood to the proof. He makes no complaints of the English Ladies."

In an issue of the same paper 9th November, of the same year, it is mentioned that the Rt. Hon. Lord Ferrars, Sir John Fielding, Messrs. Addington, Wright and other worthy magistrates and gentlemen and their ladies did the Chevalier d'Eon the honour to dine with him in Brewer St., Golden Square (common proof that the Chevalier d'Eon is not confined in the Bastille). D'Eon was much too wily and too much accustomed to attack to allow diplomatic insinuations to pass unheeded. He was now beginning to apply his garnered experience to his own protection.

From the above extract of 16th November one can note how the allegation as to his sex was beginning to rankle in the soldier's mind, and how an open threat of punishment is conveyed in diplomatic form. Indeed he had reason to take umbrage at the insinuation. More than once had attempts been made to carry him off for the purpose of settling bets by a humiliating personal scrutiny. From something of the same cause his friends on his death caused an autopsy to be made before several witnesses of position and repute. Amongst these were several surgeons including Père Elisée, First Surgeon to Louis XVIII. The medical certificate ran as follows:

"Je certifie, par le présent, avoir inspecté le corps du chevalier d'Eon, en présence de M. Adair, M. Wilson et du Père Elysée, et avoir trouvé les organs masculins parfaitement formés."

X. THE BISLEY BOY

A. PROLEGOMENON

QUEEN ELIZABETH, the last of the House of Tudor, died unmarried. Since her death in 1603, there have been revolutions in England due to varying causes, but all more or less disruptive of family memories. The son of James I had his head cut off, and after the Commonwealth which followed, Charles I's son James II, had to quit on the coming of William III, by invitation. After William's death without issue, Anne, daughter of James II, reigned for a dozen years, and was succeeded by George I, descended through the female line from James I. His descendants still sit on the throne of England.

NO DESCENDANTS

The above facts are given not merely in the way of historical enlightenment but rather as a sort of apologetic prolegomenon to the ethical consideration of the matter immediately before us. Had Queen Elizabeth had any descendants, they need not have feared any discussion of her claims of descent. The issue of the legality of her mother's marriage had been tried exhaustively both before and after her own birth, and she held the sceptre both by the will of her dead father and the consent of her dead half-sister who left no issue. But Queen Elizabeth, whatever her origin, would have been a sufficient ancestor for any King or any Dynasty. Still, had she left issue there might have been lesser people, descendants, whose feelings in the matter of personal and family pride would have required consideration; and no person entering on an analysis of historical fact would have felt quite free-handed in such an investigation.

B. THE QUEEN'S SECRET

There are quite sufficient indications throughout the early life of Queen Elizabeth that there was *some* secret which she kept religiously guarded. Various historians of the time have referred to it, and now and again in a way which is enlightening.

In a letter to the Protector Somerset in 1549, when the Princess Elizabeth was 15, Sir Robert Tyrwhitt says:

> "I do verily believe that there hath been some secret promise between my Lady, Mistress Ashley, and the Cofferer" [Sir Thomas Parry] never to confess to death, and if it be so, it will never be gotten of her, unless by the King's Majesty or else by your Grace."

In his *Girlhood of Queen Elizabeth* Mr. Frank A. Mumby writes of this:—

> "Elizabeth was as loyal to Parry as to Mrs. Ashley; she reinstated him after a year's interval, in his office as Cofferer,

and on her accession to the throne she appointed him Controller of the royal household. She continued to confer preferment upon both Parry and his daughter to the end of their lives —"conduct," remarks Miss Strickland, "which naturally induces a suspicion that secrets of great moment had been confided to him—secrets that probably would have touched not only the maiden name of his royal Mistress, but placed her life in jeopardy, and that he had preserved these inviolate. The same may be supposed with respect to Mrs. Ashley, to whom Elizabeth clung with unshaken tenacity through every storm."

Major Martin Hume in his *Courtships of Queen Elizabeth* says of the favourable treatment of the Governess and the Cofferer:—

"The confessions of Ashley and Parry are bad enough; but they probably kept back more than they told, for on Elizabeth's accession and for the rest of their lives, they were treated with marked favour. Parry was knighted and made Treasurer of the Household, and on Mrs. Ashley's death in July 1565 the Queen visited her in person and mourned her with great grief."

The same writer says elsewhere in the book:

"Lady Harrington and Mrs. Ashley were, in fact, the only ladies about the Queen who were absolutely in her confidence."

In a letter to the Doge of Venice in 1556 Giovanni Michiel wrote:

"She" [Elizabeth] "I understand, having plainly said that she will not marry, even were they to give her the King's" [Philip of Spain] "son" [Don Carlos, Philip's son by his first wife] "or find any other great prince, I again respectfully remind your serenity to enjoin secrecy about this."

Count de Feria wrote in April, 1559:

"If my spies do not lie, which I believe they do not, for a certain reason which they have recently given me, I understand that she [Elizabeth] will not bear children."

At this time Elizabeth was only 26 years of age. The following extract is taken from Mr. Mumby's *Girlhood of Queen Elizabeth* in which is given the translation taken from Leti's *La Vie d'Elizabeth.* The letter is from Princess Elizabeth to Lord Admiral Seymour, 1548 (*apropos* of his intentions regarding her):—

"It has also been said that I have only refused you because I was thinking of some one else. I therefore entreat you, my lord, to set your mind at rest on this subject, and to be persuaded by this declaration that up to this time I have not the slightest intention of being married, and, that if ever I should think of it (*which I do not believe is possible*) you would be the first to whom I should make known my resolution."

C. BISLEY

The place known to the great public as Bisley is quite other than that under present consideration. Bisley, the ground for rifle competitions, is in Surrey, thoughtfully placed in juxtaposition to an eminent cemetery. It bears every indication of newness—so far as any locality of old earth can be new.

But the other is the original place of the name, possessing a recorded history which goes back many hundreds of years. It is in Gloucestershire high up on the eastern side of the Cotswold Hills at their southern end where they rise above the Little Avon which runs into the embouchure of the Severn to the Bristol Channel. The trace of Roman occupation is all over that part of England. When the pioneers of that strenuous nation made their essay on Britain they came with the intention of staying; and to-day their splendid roads remain unsurpassed —almost unsurpassable. In this part of the West Country there are several of them, of which the chief are Irmin (or Ermine) Street, running from Southampton through Cirencester and Gloucester to Caerleon, and Ikenild Street running from Cirencester, entering Gloucestershire at Eastleach. I am particular about these roads as we may require to notice them carefully. There is really but one Bisley in this part of the country, but the name is spelled so variously that the simple phonetic spelling might well serve for a nucleating principle. In all sorts of papers, from Acts of Parliament and Royal Charters down to local deeds of tenancy, it is thus varied—Bisleigh, Bistlegh, Byselegh, Bussely. In this part of the Cotswolds "Over" is a common part of a name which was formerly used as a prefix. Such is not always at once apparent for the modern cartographer seems to prefer the modern word "upper" as the prefix. Attention is merely called to it here as later on we shall have to consider it more carefully.

The most interesting spot in the whole district is the house "Overcourt," which was once the manor-house of Bisley. It stands close to Bisley church from the grave-yard of which it is only separated by a wicket-gate. The title-deeds of this house, which is now in possession of the Gordon family show that it was a part of the dower of Queen Elizabeth. But the world went by it, and little by little the estate of which it was a portion changed hands; so that now the house remains almost as an entity. Naturally enough, the young Princess Elizabeth lived there for a time; and one can still see the room she occupied. A medium-sized room with mullioned windows, having small diamond-shaped panes set in lead after the pattern of the Tudor period. A great beam of oak, not exactly "trued" with the adze but following the natural trend of the wood, crosses the ceiling. The window looks out on a little walled-in garden, one of the flower beds of which is set in an antique stone receptacle of oblong shape which presents something of the appearance of a stone coffin of the earlier ages. Of this more anon.

Whether at the time of the birth of Elizabeth the mansion of Overcourt was itself in the King's possession is a little difficult to fathom, for, in the Confession of Thomas Parry written in 1549 concerning a period a little earlier, it is said: "And I told her" [Princess Elizabeth] "further how he" [Lord Admiral Thomas Seymour] "would have had her to have lands in Gloucestershire called Bisley as in parcel of exchange, and in Wales."

In addition to its natural desirability in the way of hygiene and altitude there seems to have been a wish on the part of family advisers of those having estates in the vicinity of this place, to enlarge their possessions. This was wise enough, for in the disturbed state of affairs which ushered in the Tudor Dynasty, and the effects of which still continued, it was of distinct benefit to have communities here and there large enough for self protection. This idea held with many of the families as well as individuals whose names are associated with Bisley. Henry VIII himself, as over-lord with ownership derived from the Norman Conquest, had feudal claims on the de Bohuns who represented all the local possessions of the Dukedom of Gloucester and the Earldoms of Essex Hereford and Northampton. Also the greedy eyes of certain strong men and families who had hopes that time and influence already existing, might later on bring them benefit, were fixed on this desirable spot. Thomas Seymour, the unscrupulous brother of the future Lord Protector, was high in influence in the early days of the Princess Elizabeth, and even then must have had ambitious designs of marrying her. On the death of Henry VIII he had, when Lord Sudeley, married the king's widow within a few months of her widowhood, and received a grant of the royal possession at Bisley which, on his attainder, passed on to Sir Anthony Kingston, who doubtless had already marked it down as an objective of his cupidity.

The "Hundred of Bisley" was one of the seven of Cirencester which of old were farmed by the Abbey of Tewksbury. Its position was so full of possibilities of future development as to justify the acquisitive spirit of those who desired it. In its bounds were what is now the town of Stroud, as well as a whole line of mills which had in early days great effect as they were workable by both wind and water power, both of which were to be had in profusion. This little remote hamlet had a progressive industry of its own in the shape of a manufacture of woollen cloths. It also represented dyeing in scarlet and was the place of origin of Giles Gobelin, a famous dyer who gave his name to the Gobelin tapestry.

One other thing must be distinctly borne in mind regarding Bisley in the first half of the sixteenth century; it was comparatively easy of access from London for those who wished to go there. A line drawn on the map will show that on the way as *points d'appui,* were Oxford and Cirencester, both of which were surrounded with good roads as became their importance as centres. This line seems very short for its importance. To-day the journey is that of a morning; and even in the time of

Henry VIII when horse traction was the only kind available, the points were not very distant as to time of traverse. To Henry, who commanded everything and had a myriad agents eager to display their energy in his service, all was simple; and when he went a-hunting in the forests which made a network far around Berkeley Castle his objective could be easily won between breakfast and supper. There was not any difficulty therefore, and not too much personal strain, when he chose to visit his little daughter even though at the start one should be at Nether Lypiat and the other at Greenwich or Hatfield or Eltham.

D. THE TRADITION

The Tradition is that the little Princess Elizabeth, during her childhood, was sent away with her governess for change of air to Bisley where the strong sweet air of the Cotswold Hills would brace her up. The healthy qualities of the place were known to her father and many others of those around her. Whilst she was at Overcourt, word was sent to her governess that the King was coming to see his little daughter; but shortly before the time fixed, and whilst his arrival was expected at any hour, a frightful catastrophe happened. The child, who had been ailing in a new way, developed acute fever, and before steps could be taken even to arrange for her proper attendance and nursing, she died. The governess feared to tell her father—

Henry VIII had the sort of temper which did not make for the happiness of those around him. In her despair she, having hidden the body, rushed off to the village to try to find some other child whose body could be substituted for that of the dead princess so that the evil moment of disclosure of the sad fact might be delayed till after His Majesty's departure. But the population was small and no girl child of any kind was available. The distracted woman then tried to find a living girl child who could be passed off for the princess, whose body could be hidden away for the time.

Throughout the little village and its surroundings was to be found no girl child of an age reasonably suitable for the purpose required. More than ever distracted, for time was flying by, she determined to take the greater risk of a boy substitute—if a boy could be found. Happily for the poor woman's safety, for her very life now hung in the balance, this venture was easy enough to begin. There *was* a boy available, and just such a boy as would suit the special purpose for which he was required—a boy well known to the governess, for the little Princess had taken a fancy to him and had lately been accustomed to play with him. Moreover, he was a pretty boy as might have been expected from the circumstance of the little Lady Elizabeth having chosen him as her playmate. He was close at hand and available. So he was clothed in the dress of the dead child, they being of about equal stature; and when the King's fore-rider appeared the poor overwrought governess was able to breathe freely.

The visit passed off successfully. Henry suspected nothing; as the whole thing had happened so swiftly, there had been no antecedent anxiety. Elizabeth had been brought up in such dread of her father that he had not, at the rare intervals of his seeing her, been accustomed to any affectionate effusiveness on her part; and in his hurried visit he had no time for baseless conjecture.

Then came the natural nemesis of such a deception. As the dead could not be brought back to life, and as the imperious monarch, who bore no thwarting of his wishes, was under the impression that he could count on his younger daughter as a pawn in the great game of political chess which he had entered on so deeply, those who by now must have been in the secret did not and could not dare to make disclosure. Moreover the difficulties and dangers to one and all involved would of necessity grow with each day that passed. Willy nilly they must go on. Fortunately for the safety of their heads circumstances favoured them. The secret was, up to now, hidden in a remote village high up on the side of the Cotswold hills. Steep declivities guarded it from casual intrusion, and there was no trade beyond that occasional traffic necessary for a small agricultural community. The whole country as far as the eye could see was either royal domain or individual property owned or held by persons attached to the dynasty by blood or interest.

Facilities of intercommunication were few and slow; and above all uncertain and therefore not to be relied on.

This then was the beginning of the tradition which has existed locally ever since. In such districts change is slow, and what has been may well be taken, unless there be something to the contrary, for what is. The isolation of the hamlet in the Cotswolds where the little princess lived for a time—and is supposed to have died—is almost best exemplified by the fact that though the momentous secret has existed for between three and four centuries, no whisper of it has reached the great world without its confines. Not though the original subject of it was the very centre of the wildest and longest battle which has ever taken place since the world began—polemical, dynastic, educational, international, commercial. Anyone living in any town in our own age, where advance and expansiveness are matters of degree, not of fact, may find it hard to believe that any such story, nebulous though it may be, could exist unknown and unrecorded outside a place so tiny that its most important details will not be found even on the ordnance map of an inch to the mile. But a visit to Bisley will set aside any such doubts. The place itself has hardly changed, in any measure to be apparent as a change, in the three centuries and more. The same buildings stand as of yore; the same estate wall, though more picturesque with lichen, and with individual stones corrugated by weather and dislocated by arboreal growths, speak of an epoch ending with the Tudor age. The doors of the great tithe-barns which remain as souvenirs of extinct feudalism, still yawn wide on their festered hinges. Nay, even the very trees show amongst their ranks an extraordinary percentage of giants which have withstood unimpaired all the changes that have been.

Leaving busy and thriving Stroud, one climbs the long hill past Lipiat and emerges in the village, where time has suddenly ceased, and we find ourselves in the age and the surroundings which saw the House of York fade into the Tudor dynasty. Such a journey is almost a necessity for a proper understanding of the story of the Bisley Boy, which has by the effluxion of time attained to almost the grace and strength of a legend. It is quite possible that though the place has stood still, the tradition has not, for it is in the nature of intellectual growth to advance. One must not look on the Gloucestershire people as sleepy—sleepiness is no characteristic of that breezy upland; but dreaming, whether its results be true or false, does not depend on sleep. In cases like the present, sleep is not to be looked on as a blood relation of death but rather as a preservative against the ravages of time—like the mysterious slumber of King Arthur and others who are destined for renewal.

It may be taken for granted that in course of time and under the process of purely oral communication, the story told in whispers lost nothing in the way of romance or credibility; that flaws or lacunæ were made good by inquiry; and that recollections of overlooked or forgotten facts were recalled or even supplemented by facile invention. But it may also be taken for granted that no statement devoid of a solid foundation could become permanently accepted. There were too many critics around, with memories unimpaired by overwork, to allow incorrect statements to pass unchallenged. There is always this in tradition, that the collective mind which rules in small communities is a child's mind, which must ever hold grimly on to fact. And that behind the child's mind is the child's nature which most delights in the recountal of what it knows, and is jealous of any addition to the story which is a part of its being.

Major Martin Hume writes in his *Courtships of Queen Elizabeth:*

"Elizabeth was only three when her mother's fall removed her from the line of the succession. . . . In 1542, however, the death of James V of Scotland and the simultaneous birth of his daughter Mary seemed to bring nearer Henry's idea of a union between the two crowns. He proposed to marry the baby Queen of Scots to his infant son and at the same time he offered the hand of Elizabeth (then nine) to a son of Arran—head of House of Hamilton, next heir to the Scottish crown. . . . Mary and Elizabeth were restored to their places in the line of succession. . . . In January 1547 Henry VIII died, leaving the succession to his two daughters in tail after Edward VI and his heirs. Queen Catherine (Parr) immediately married Sir Thomas Seymour, brother of Protector Somerset and uncle of the little king (Edward VI). To them was confided Princess Elizabeth then a girl of 14.'"

Elizabeth was three in 1536. The story of the Bisley Boy dates probably to 1543–4. So that if the story have any foundation at all in fact, signs of a complete change of identity in the person of Princess Elizabeth must be looked for in the period of some seven or eight years which intervened.

E. THE DIFFICULTY OF PROOF

In such a case as that before us the difficulty of proof is almost insuperable. But fortunately we are dealing with a point not of law but of history. Proof is not in the first instance required, but only surmise, to be followed by an argument of probability. Such records as still exist are all the proofs that can be adduced; and all we can do is to search for such records as still exist, without which we lack the enlightenment that waits on discovery. In the meanwhile we can deduce a just conclusion from such materials as we do possess. Failing certitude, which is under the circumstances almost impossible, we only arrive at probability; and with that until discovery of more reliable material we must be content.

Let us therefore sum up: first the difficulties of the task before us; then the enlightenments. "Facts," says one of the characters of Charles Dickens, "bein' stubborn and not easy drove," are at least, so far as they go, available. We are free to come to conclusions and to make critical comments. Our risk is that if we err—on whichever side does not matter—we reverse our position and become ourselves the objects of attack.

Our main difficulties are two. First, that all from whom knowledge might have been obtained are dead and their lips are closed; second, that records are incomplete. This latter is the result of one of two causes—natural decay or purposed obliteration. The tradition of the Bisley Boy has several addenda due to time and thought. One of these is that some of those concerned in the story disappeared from the scene.

The story runs that on Elizabeth's accession or under circumstances antecedent to it all who were in the secret and still remained were "got rid of." The phrase is a convenient one and not unknown in history. Fortunately those who *must* have been in such a secret—if there was one—were but few. If such a thing occurred in reality, four persons were necessarily involved in addition to Elizabeth herself: (1) Mrs. Ashley, (2) Thomas Parry, (3) the parent of the living child who replaced the dead one; the fourth, being an unknown quantity, represents an idea rather than a person—a nucleated identity typical of family life with attendant difficulties of concealment. Of these four—three real persons and an idea—three are accounted for, so far as the "got rid of" theory is concerned. Elizabeth never told; Thomas Parry and Mrs. Ashley remained silent, in the full confidence of the (supposed) Princess who later was Queen. With regard to the last, the nucleated personality which includes the unknown parent possibly but not of certainty, contemporary record is silent; and we can only regard him or her as a mysterious entity available for conjecture in such cases of difficulty as may present themselves.

We must perforce, therefore, fall back on pure unadulterated probability, based on such rags of fact as can be produced at our inquest. Our comfort—content being an impossibility—must lie in the generally-accepted aphorism; "Truth will prevail." In real life it is not always so; but it is a comforting belief and may remain *faut de mieux.*

A grave cause of misleading is inexact translation—whether the fault be in ignorance or intentional additions to or substractions from text referred to. A case in point is afforded by the letter already referred to from Leti's *La Vie d'Elizabeth.* In the portion quoted Elizabeth mentioned her intention of not marrying: "I have not the slightest intention of being married, and

. . . if ever I should think of it *(which I do not believe is possible).*" Now in Mr. Mumby's book the quotation is made from Leti's *La Vie d'Elizabeth* which is the translation into French from the original Italian, the passage marked above in italics is simply: "ce que je ne crois pas." The addition of the words "is possible" gives what is under the circumstances quite a different meaning to the earliest record we have concerning the very point we are investigating. When I began this investigation, I looked on the passage—neither Mumby, remember, nor even Leti, but what professed to be the *ipsissima verba* of Elizabeth herself—and I was entirely misled until I had made comparison for myself—*Quis custodiet ipsos custodes?* The addition of the two words, which seems at first glance merely to emphasise an expression of opinion, changes the meaning of the writer to a belief so strong that the recital of it gives it the weight of intention. Under ordinary circumstances this would not matter much; but as we have to consider it in the light of a man defending his head against danger, and in a case where absolute circumspection is a necessary condition of safety so that intention becomes a paramount force, exactness of expression is all-important.

The only way to arrive at probability is to begin with fact. Such is a base for even credulity or its opposite, and if it is our wish or intention to be just there need be no straining on either one side or the other. In the case of the Bisley Boy the points to be considered are:

1. The time at which the change was or could be affected.

2. The risk of discovery, (a) at first, (b) afterwards.

It will be necessary to consider these separately for manifest reasons. The first belongs to the region of Danger; the second to the region of Difficulty, with the headsman's axe glittering ominously in the background.

F. THE TIME AND THE OPPORTUNITY

(*a*) *The time at which the change was or could have been effected.*

For several valid reasons I have come to the conclusion that the crucial period by which the Bisley story must be tested is the year ending with July 1544. No other time either earlier or later would, so far as we know, have fulfilled the necessary conditions.

First of all the question of sex has to be considered; and it is herein that, lacking suitable and full opportunity, discovery of such an imposture must have been at once detected—certainly had it commenced at an early age. In babyhood the whole of the discipline of child-life begins. The ordinary cleanliness of life has to be taught, and to this end there is no portion of the infantile body which is not subject to at least occasional inspection. This disciplinary inspection lasts by force of habit until another stage on the journey towards puberty has been reached. Commercial use in America fixes stages of incipient womanhood—by dry goods' advertisement—as "children's, misses' and girls' clothing," and the illustration will sufficiently serve. It seems at first glance an almost unnecessary intrusion into purely domestic life; but the present is just one of those cases where the experience of women is not only useful but necessary. In a question of identity of sex the nursemaid and the washerwoman play useful parts in the witness box. Regarding Elizabeth's childhood no question need ever or can ever arise. For at least the first ten years of her life, a woman's sex *need* not be known outside the nursery and the sick room; but then this is the very time when her attendants have direct and ample knowledge. Moreover in the case of the child of Queen Anne (Boleyn) there was every reason why the sex should have been unreservedly known. Henry VIII divorced Katherine of Aragon and married Anne in the hope of having legitimate male issue to sit on the throne of England. Later, when both Katherine and Anne had failed to satisfy him as to male issue, he divorced Anne and married Jane Seymour for the same purpose. In the interval either his views had enlarged or his patience had extended; for, when Jane's life hung in the balance, owing to an operation which the surgeons considered necessary, and the husband was consulted as to which life they should, in case of needful choice, try to save, his reply was peculiar—though, taken in the light of historical perspective, not at variance with his dominating idea. Gregorio Leti thus describes the incident (the quotation is made from the translation of the Italian into French and published in Amsterdam in 1694):—

"Quand les médécins demandèrent au Roi qui l'on sauverait de la mère ou de l'enfant, il répondit, qu'il auroit extremement souhait de pouvoir sauver la mère et l'enfant, mais que cel n'étant possible, il vouloit que l'on sauvat l'enfant plutôt que la mère parce qu'il trouveroit assez d' autres femmes."

It had become a monomania with Henry that he should be father of a lawful son; and when the child of his second union was expected, he so took the consummation of his wishes for granted that those in attendance on his wife were actually afraid to tell him the truth. It would have been fortune and social honour to whosoever should bear him the glad tidings. We may be sure then that news so welcome would never have been perverted by those who had so much to gain. As it was, the "lady-mistress"—as she called herself—of the little Princess, Mrs. (afterwards Lady) Bryan, wrote in her letter to Lord Cromwell in 1536—Elizabeth being then in her third year:—

"She is as toward a child and as gentle of conditions, as ever I knew any in my life."

The writer could have had no ignorance as to the sex of the child, for in the same letter she gives Cromwell a list of her wants in the way of clothing; which list is of the most intimate kind, including gown, kirtle, petticoat, "no manner of linen nor smocks," kerchiefs, rails, body stitchets, handkerchiefs, sleeves, mufflers, biggens. As in the same letter it is mentioned that the women attending the child were under the rule of Lady Bryan—an accomplished nurse who had brought up Princess Mary and had been "governess to the children his Grace have had ever since"—it can be easily understood she was well acquainted with even the smallest detail of the royal nursery. Had the trouble of the lady-mistress been with regard to superabundance of underclothing, one might have understood ignorance on the part of the responsible controller; but in the plentiful lack of almost every garment necessary for the child's wear by day or by night there could be no question as to her ostensible sex at this age.

Thence on, there were experienced and devoted persons round the little Princess, whose value in her father's eyes was largely enhanced since he had secured, for the time, her legitimacy by an Act of Parliament.

After Elizabeth had been legitimised, she became one of the pieces in the gigantic game of chess on which Henry had embarked. Despite the fact that the son for whom he had craved was now a boy of six, it was only wise to consider and be prepared for whatever might happen in case Prince Edward should not live, and if, in such a case, Mary should die without issue. The case was one of amazing complexity, and as the time wore on the religious question became structurally involved. England had declared in no uncertain voice in favour of Protestantism, and the whole forces of Rome were arrayed against her. Mary was altogether in favour of the religion of her injured mother, and behind her stood the power of Catholicism which, even in that unscrupulous age, was well ahead in the race of unscrupulousness. And as Elizabeth stood next to the young Prince Edward in the forces of Reformation, on her was focussed much of the suspicion of polemic intrigue. The papacy was all powerful in matters of secret inquiry. Indeed in such an inquest its powers were unique, for unscrupulous spies were everywhere—even, it was alleged, in the confessional. How then could such a secret as the sex of a little girl of not a dozen years of age, who was constantly surrounded by women necessarily conversant with every detail of her life, be kept from all who wished to solve it. In such a state of affairs suspicion was equivalent to discovery. And discovery meant ruin to all concerned, death to abettors of the fraud, woe and destruction to England and a general upheaval of the fundamental ideas of Christendom. It may, I presume, be taken for granted without flaw or mitigation of any kind that up to July, 1543, the "Princess Elizabeth" was what she appeared to be—a girl.

At the time of her first letter to the new Queen, Catherine (Parr), she was just a trifle under ten years of age and a well-grown child, quick, clever, rather precocious, and well grounded in the learning of her time. The exact date of this letter is not given by Leti—of which more anon—but it must have been somewhere between July 12 and 31, 1543. Henry VIII married Catherine Parr on 12 July, and in her letter of 1543 Elizabeth calls Catherine "your Majesty." In her letter of 31 July, 1544 she writes to the same correspondent:

> " . . . has deprived me for a whole year of your most illustrious presence."

The whereabouts of Elizabeth during this last year appears to be the centre of the mystery; and if any letter or proof is ever found of Elizabeth's being anywhere but in her own house of Overcourt in Bisley Parish, it will go far to settle the vexed question now brought before the world for the first time.

(*b*) *The opportunity*

The year 1542 was a busy time for Henry VIII. He had on hand, either pending or going on, two momentous wars, one with Scotland the other with France. The causes of either of these were too complicated for mention here; suffice it to say that they were chiefly dynastic and polemic. In addition he was busy with matrimonial matters, chiefly killing off his fifth wife Catherine Howard, and casting eyes on the new-made widow of Lord Latimer. In 1543 he married the lady, as his sixth wife. She herself can hardly be said to have lacked matrimonial experience, as this was her third union. Her first venture was with the elderly Lord Borough, who, like Lord Latimer, left her wealthy. Henry had by now got what might be called in the slang of the time "the marriage habit," and honeymoon dalliance had hardly the same charm for him as it usually is supposed to have with those blessed with a lesser succession of spouses. The consequence was that he was able to give more attention to the necessary clearing up of the Scottish war, which finished at Solway Moss on December 14th, with the consequent death from chagrin of the Scottish King James V. The cause of the war, however, continued in the shape of a war with France which went on till 1546 when peace was declared to the pecuniary benefit of the English King. For the last two years of this time Henry carried on the war singlehanded, as the Emperor Charles V, who had begun it as his ally, withdrew.

There is a paragraph in Grafton's *Chronicle* published in 1569 which throws a flood of light on Elizabeth's absence at this time, 1543: "This yeare was in London a great death of the pestilence, and therefore Mighelmas terme was adjourned to Saint Albones, and there it was kept to the ende."

In his *Girlhood of Queen Elizabeth,* Mr. Mumby says: "For some obscure reason Elizabeth seems to have fallen out of her father's favour again very soon after Catherine Parr had obtained his consent to her return to Court" (1543). No such cause for the removal of the Princess from London was necessary. It was probably to the presence of the pestilence in London that her removal to a remote and healthy place was due. Failing Prince Edward, then only five years of age and a weakly child, the crown must—unless some constitutional revolution be effected in the meantime or some future son be born to him—devolve on his female heirs, a matter pregnant with strife of unknown dimensions. Mary was now twenty-seven years old and of a type that did not promise much for maternity. At the same time, Mary, though his eldest living daughter, was the hope of the Catholic party, to which he was in violent opposition; whereas in Elizabeth lay the hope of the whole of the party of the Reformation. Her life was to her father far beyond the calls of parental affection or dynastic ambition, and she had to be saved at all costs from risk of health. Henry's own experience of child-life was a bitter one. Of his five children by Catherine of Aragon only one, Mary, survived childhood. Elizabeth was the only survivor of Anne Boleyn; Edward, of Jane Seymour. Anne of Cleves had no children, and if report spoke truly no chance of having any. Catherine Howard was executed childless. And he had only just married Catherine Parr, who had already had two husbands.

On July 12, 1543, Henry married Catherine and in due course devoted himself to the war. On the 14 July, 1544, he crossed from Dover to Calais to look after the conduct of affairs for himself, and on the 26th began the siege of Boulogne. This lasted for two months when having reduced the city he returned home. On the 8 September he wrote to his wife to that effect. During his absence Queen Catherine was vicegerent and had manifestly as much public work on hand as she could cope with. Bisley was a long way from London, and there were no organised posts in the sixteenth century. Moreover, ever since his last marriage, Henry had been an invalid. He was now fifty-two years of age, of unhealthy body, and so heavy that he had to be lifted by machinery. Catherine was a devoted wife; and as Henry was both violent and irritable she had little time at command to give to the affairs of other people. There was small opportunity for any one then who was sufficiently in the focus of affairs to be cognisant of such an imposture as the tradition points out. Doubtless hereafter, when a story so fascinating and at first glance so incredible begins to be examined and its details thoroughly threshed out, more items of evidence or surmise than are at present available will be found for the settlement of the question, one way or the other. In the meantime, be it remembered, that we are only examining offhand a tradition made known for the first time after three centuries. Our present business is to consider *possibilities.* Later on the time may come—as it surely will; if the story can in the least be accepted—for the consideration of *probabilities.* Both of these tentative examinations will lead to the final examination of possibility, of probability, and of proof *pro* or *contra.*

At this stage we must admit that neither time nor opportunity present any difficulty in itself insuperable.

G. THE IDENTITY OF ELIZABETH

(*a*) *Documents*

The next matter with which we have to deal is regarding the identity of Elizabeth. This needs (if necessary) a consideration of the facts of her life, and so far as we can realise them, from external appearance, mental and moral attitudes, and intentions. On account of space we must confine this branch of the subject to the smallest portion of time necessary to form any sort of just conclusion and accepting the available records up to 1543, take the next period from that time to anywhere within the first few years of her reign—by which time her character was finally fixed and the policy on which her place in history is to be judged had been formulated and tested.

This implies in the first instance a brief (very brief) study of her physique with a corollary in the shape of a few remarks on her heredity:

Grafton's Chronicle states, under the date of 7 September 1533, "the Queene was delivered of a fayre Lady" which was his Courtly way of announcing the birth of a female princess, blond in colour. In all chronicles "fayre" means of light colour. In Wintown the reputed father of Macbeth—the Devil—is spoken of as a "fayre" man; evil qualities were in that age attributed to blondes.

In a letter dated from Greenwich Palace, 18 April, 1534, Sir William Kingston said to Lord Lisle: "To-day, the King and Queen were at Eltham" (where the royal nursery then was) "and saw my Lady Princess—as goodly a child as hath been seen. Her Grace is much in the King's favour as a goodly child should be—God save her!"

In 1536, when Elizabeth was but three years old, Lady Bryan, the "Lady-mistress" of both Mary and her half-sister, wrote from Hunsdon to Lord Cromwell regarding the baby princess. "For she is as toward a child and as gentle of conditions, as ever I knew any in my life. Jesus preserve her Grace!" In the same letter she says "Mr. Shelton would have my Lady Elizabeth to dine and sup every day at the board of estate. Alas! my Lord it is not meet for a child of her age to keep such rule yet. I promise you, my lord, I dare not take it upon me to keep her Grace in health an' she keep that rule. For there she shall see divers meats, and fruits, and wines, which it would be hard for me to restrain her Grace from. Ye know, my lord, there is no place of correction there; and she is yet too young to correct greatly."

Testimony is borne according to Leti to the good qualities of the Princess Elizabeth in these early years, by the affectionate regard in which she was held by two of Henry's queens, the wronged and unhappy Anne of Cleves and the happy-natured Catherine Parr. Anne, he says, though she had only seen her twice loved her much; she thought her beautiful and full of spirit ("pleine d'esprit.") Catherine, according to the same writer who had seen her often before her marriage to Henry, admired her "esprit et ses manières."

If Leti could only have spoken at first hand, his record of her would be very valuable. But unhappily he was only born nearly thirty years after her death. His history was manifestly written from records and as Elizabeth's fame was already made before he began to treat of her his work is largely a panegyric of hearsay. There is, regarding the youth of the Princess, such an overdone flood of adulation that it is out of place in a serious history of a human life. In his account of the time which we are considering, we find the child compared in both matters of body and mind to an angel. She is credited at the age of ten with an amount of knowledge in all branches of learning sufficient to equip the illustrious men of a century. The fact is the Italian has accepted the queen's great position, and then reconstructed her youth to accord with it, in such a way as to show that whatever remarkable abilities she possessed were the direct outcome of her own natural qualities.[1]

The details above given are not merely meagre but are only explicable by the fact that during the earlier years of her life the child was not considered of any importance. The circumstances of Anne's marriage—which in any case was delayed till it became a necessary preliminary to the legitimacy on which any future claim to the throne must rest—did not make for a belief in the public mind for its permanency. Things were fluctuating in the religious world and few were inclined to the belief that the Pope (with whom lay the last word and whose political leanings in favour of Catherine of Aragon and the validity of her marriage to Henry were well known) would be overthrown by the English King. And in any case, were Henry

[1] Amongst other branches of knowledge he credits her with knowing well "Geography, Cosmography, Mathematics, Architecture, Painting, Arithmetic, History, Mechanics." She had a special facility in learning languages; spoke and wrote French, Italian, Spanish, Flemish. She loved poetry and wrote it, but regarded it as a useless amusement and, as it was distasteful to her, turned to history and politics. Finally he adds: "She was naturally ambitious and always knew how to hide her defects."

to be the final judge of appeal in his own case no great continuity of purpose could be expected from him. The first important event which we have to consider with reference to the question before us is Elizabeth's first letter to Queen Catherine (Parr) in 1543. In this the girl then ten years old writes to her new step-mother, at whose marriage she together with her half-sister Mary had been present. It is in form a dutiful letter, not entirely without an apparent compulsion or at least intelligent supervision. As it stands, it is impossible to believe that it emanated from a child of ten quite free to follow out its inclinations. The dutifulness is altogether, or largely, due to the training and self-suppression of the royal child of an arbitrary father with absolute power. But it remains for each reader to consider it impartially. The points which we should do well to note here are its plain form of expression, and its entire absence of personal affection. The latter is all the more marked in that it was a letter of thanks for a kindness conferred. Elizabeth was very anxious to come to her father, and Catherine had furthered her wish and secured its fulfilment. After the marriage, the child, as is shown (or rather inferred), had been sent away for more than a year, which absence had been prolonged for at least six months—as already shown.

There is little evidence of Elizabeth's inner nature in these early days; but we have every right to think that she was of a peaceable, kindly and affectionate nature. Lady Bryan her first nurse or governess (after Lady Boleyn, Anne's mother) thought highly of her. Catherine Ashley, who had charge of her next, loved her and was her devoted servant, friend and confidant till her death.

Thomas Parry her life-long friend was devoted to her, and when the circumstances of their respective lives and the happenings of the time kept them apart, she restored him at the first opportunity and made his fortune her special care.

There is little base here on which to build an inverted pyramid; our only safety is in taking things as they seem to be and using common sense.

(*b*) *Changes*

Let us now take the years beginning with 1544. From this time on, more is known of the personality of Elizabeth; in fact there is little unknown, that is, of matters of fact, and to this only we must devote ourselves. Whatever may have been Elizabeth's motives we can only infer them. She was a secretive person and took few into her confidence, unless it was of vital necessity—and then only in matters required by the circumstance. The earliest knowledge we have of this second period of her history is in her letter to Queen Catherine (Parr) written from St. James' Palace on 31 July, 1544.

In the year which had elapsed since her last recorded letter Elizabeth's literary style had entirely changed. The meagre grudging style has become elegant and even florid with the ornate grace and imagery afforded by the study of the Latin and French tongues. Altogether there is not merely a more accomplished diction but there is behind it a truer feeling and larger sympathy. It is more in accord with the letter accompanying the gift to the Queen, of her translation of the *Mirror of the Sinful Soul* which she had dedicated to her.

Historians have given various rescripts of certain earlier letters of the Princess Elizabeth, but none of them seem in harmony of thought with this, whereas it is quite in accord with her later writings. Metabolism is an accepted doctrine of physiology; but its scope is not—as yet at all events—extended to the intellect, and we must take things as we find them within the limits of human knowledge.

It will perhaps be as well to reserve the consideration of any other point, except the change in actual identity, till the complete analogy of all natural processes is an established fact.

(*c*) *Her personality*

We have no letters of Princess Elizabeth before 1543 which are not open to grave doubt as to date, but there is one letter to which allusion must almost of necessity be made. It is a letter from Roger Ascham, tutor to the Princess Elizabeth, to

Mrs. Ashley. No date is given by Mr. Mumby, but he states in his text that it was written "during Grindal's term of office" as tutor to the Princess. Mumby quotes from the *Elizabeth* of Miss Strickland, who in turn quotes from Whittaker's *Richmondshire.* Now Grindal's term of office lasted from 1546 (probably the end of that year) till it was cut short by his death from the Plague in 1548, so that he could not have known his royal pupil *before* 1544. The text of the letter leads a careful reader to infer that it was written *after* that date. The important part of the letter is as follows:

" . . . the thanks you have deserved from that noble imp by your labour and wisdom now flourishing in all goodly godliness. . . . I wish her Grace (Elizabeth) to come to that end in perfectness and likelihood of her wit and painlessness in her study, true trade of her teaching, which your diligent overseeing doth most constantly promise. . . . I wish all increase of virtue and honour to that my good lady, whose wit, good Mrs. Ashley, I beeseech you somewhat favour. Blunt edges be dull and dure much pain to little profit; the free edge is soon turned if it be not handled thereafter. If you pour much drink at once into a goblet, the most part will dash out and run over; if ye pour it softly you may fill it even to the top, and so her Grace, I doubt not, by little and little may be increased in learning, that at length greater cannot be required."

If this letter means anything at all—which in the case of such a man as Roger Ascham is not to be doubted—it means that Mrs. Ashley, then her governess, was cautioned not to press the little girl overmuch in her lessons. It is an acknowledgment of the teacher's zeal as well as affection, and in the flowery and involved style of the period and the man, illustrates the theory by pointing out the error of trying to fill a small vessel from a larger one by pouring too fast. She is not a backward child, he says in effect, but go slowly with her education, you cannot give full learning all at once.

Compare this letter with that of the same writer to John Sturmius, Rector of the Protestant University of Strasbourg, on the same subject in 1550:

"The Lady Elizabeth has accomplished her sixteenth year; and so much of solidity of understanding, such courtesy united with dignity, have never been observed at so early an age. She has the most ardent love of true religion and of the best kind of literature. The constitution of her mind is exempt from female weakness, and she is endued with a masculine power of application.

"No apprehension can be quicker than hers, no memory more retentive. French and Italian she speaks like English; Latin with fluency, propriety and judgment; she also spoke Greek with me, frequently, willingly, and understanding well. Nothing can be more elegant than her handwriting, whether in the Greek or Roman character. In music she is very skilful but does not greatly delight. With respect to personal decoration, she greatly prefers a simple elegance to show and splendour, so despising the outward adorning of plaiting the hair and of wearing of gold, that in the whole manner of her life she rather resembles Hippolyta than Phædra."

That such a scholar as Roger Ascham makes the simile is marked. Hippolyta was a Queen of the

Amazons and Phædra was an almost preternaturally womanly woman, one with a tragic intensity of passion.

The Elizabeth whom we know from 1544 to 1603 certainly had brains enough to protect her neck. In 1549 Sir Robert Tyrwhitt wrote to the Protector Somerset, apropos of the strenuous effort being made to gain from her some admission damaging to herself concerning Thomas Seymour's attempts to win her hand:

"She hath a very pretty wit and nothing is gotten out of her but by great policy."

In a letter from Simon Renard Ambassador to the Emperor Charles V dated London September 23, 1553, there is incidentally a statement regarding Elizabeth's character which it is wise to hold in mind when discussing this particular period of her history. Writing of Elizabeth's first attendance at Mass he said: "she, Mary, . . . entreated Madame Elizabeth to speak freely of all that was on her conscience, to which the Princess replied that she was resolved to declare publicly that in going to Mass as in all else that she had done, she had only obeyed the voice of her conscience; and that she had acted freely, without fear, deceit, or pretence. We have since been told, however, that the said Lady Elizabeth is very timid, and that while she was speaking with the Queen she trembled very much."

Compare with this the letter of 16th March, 1554

to the Queen (Mary) written just as she was told to go to the Tower. In this letter which is beautifully written and with not a trace of agitation she protests her innocence of any plot. Her mental attitude was thoroughly borne out by a calm dignity of demeanour which is more in accord with male than female nature. In very fact Elizabeth appears all her life since 1544 to have been playing with great thoughtfulness and yet dexterity a diplomatic game—acting with histrionic subtlety a part which she had chosen advisedly.

A good idea of the personality of Elizabeth during the period beginning with 1544 may be had from a brief consideration of the risks which a person taking up such an imposture would run, first at the time of beginning the venture and then of sustaining the undertaken rôle. At the outset a boy of ten or eleven would not think of taking it seriously. At first he would look on it as a "lark" and carry out the idea with a serious energy only known in play-time. Later thought would give it a new charm in the shape of danger. This, while adding to his great zest, would sober him; thence on it would be a game—just such a game as a boy loves, perpetual struggle to get the best of someone else. To some natures wit against wit is a better strife than strength against strength, and if one were well equipped for such a fray the game would satisfy the ambition of his years. In any case when once such a game was entered on, the stake would be his own head—a consideration which must undoubtedly make for strenuous effort—even in boyhood.

The task which would have followed—which did follow if the Bisley story is true—would have been vastly greater. If the imposture escaped immediate detection—which is easily conceivable—a new kind of endeavour would have been necessary; one demanding the utmost care and perpetual vigilance in addition to the personal qualities necessary for the carrying out of the scheme. Little help could be given to the young boy on whom rested the weight of what must have appeared to all concerned in it a stupendous undertaking. From the nature of the task, which was one which even the faintest breath of suspicion would have ruined, the little band, originally involved, could gain no assistance. Safety was only possible by the maintenance of the most rigid secrecy. All around them were enemies served by a host of zealous spies. If then the story be true, those who carried such an enterprising situation to lasting success, must have been no common persons. Let us suppose for a moment that the story was true. In such case the Boy of Bisley who acted the part of the Princess Elizabeth could have had only two assistants—assistants even if they were only passive. *Whatever* may have happened we know from history that both Mrs. Ashley and Thomas Parry were ingrainedly loyal to Elizabeth, as she was to them.

For convenience we shall speak of the substitute of the Princess as though he were the Princess herself whom he appeared to be, and for whom he was accepted thenceforth. That the imposture—if there was one—succeeded is a self-evident fact; for almost sixty years there was no question raised by any person of either sex and of any political opinion. The statecraft of England, France, the Papacy, and the German Empire were either unsuspicious or in error—or both. It is reasonable to imagine that a person of strong character and active intelligence might have steered deftly between these variously opposing forces. It is conceivable that in the case of a few individuals there might have been stray fragmentary clouds of suspicion; though if there were any they must have come to those who were held to a consequent inactivity by other dominating causes. We shall have occasion presently to touch on this subject but in the meantime we must accept it that there was no opinion expressed by any one in such a way as necessarily to provoke action. Of course after a time even suspicion became an impossibility. Here was a young girl growing into womanhood whom all around her had known all her life—or what was equivalent—believed they had. It is only now after three centuries that we can consider who it was that formed the tally of those who knew the personality of Elizabeth during both periods of her youth, that up to 1543–4 and that which followed.

Henry VIII manifestly not only had no doubt on the subject but no thought. If he had had he was just the man to have settled it at once. Anne Boleyn was dead, so was her predecessor in title. Anne of Cleves had accepted the annulment of her marriage—and a pension. Jane Seymour and Catherine Howard were both dead. Nearly all those who as nurses, governesses, or teachers, Lady Bryan, Richard Croke, William Grindal, Roger Ascham, who knew the first period were dead or had retired into other spheres. Those who remained knowing well the individuality of the Princess and representing both periods were Mrs. Ashley, Thomas Parry and the Queen (later dowager) Catherine Parr.

We know already of the faithfulness of the two former, the man who was a clever as well as a faithful servant, and the woman, who having no children of her own, took to her heart the little child entrusted to her care and treated her with such affectionate staunchness—a staunchness which has caused more than one historian to suspect that there was some grave secret between them which linked their fortunes together.

As to Catherine Parr we are able to judge from her letters that she was fond of her step-daughter and was consistently kind to her. Those who choose to study the matter further can form an opinion of their own from certain recorded episodes which, given without any elucidating possibilities leave the historians in further doubt. Leti puts in his *Life,* under the date of 1543, "before her marriage to Henry, Catherine Parr had seen often Elizabeth and admired her." The Italian historian *may* have had some authority for the statement; but also it may have been taken from some statement made by Elizabeth in later years or by some person in her interest, to create a misleading belief. In any case let us accept the statement as a matter of fact. If so it may throw a light on another branch of this eternal and diverse mystery. Martin Hume and F. A. Mumby approaching the subject from different points confess themselves puzzled by Elizabeth's attitude to men. The former writes in his *Courtships of Queen Elizabeth*:

> "No one can look at the best portraits of Elizabeth without recognising at a glance that she was not a sensual woman. The lean, austere face, the tight thin lips, the pointed delicate chin, the cold dull eyes, tell of a character the very opposite of lascivious."

Mr. Mumby writing about Mrs. Ashley's "Confession" and of the horse-play between Elizabeth and Lord Seymour (whom Queen Catherine had married immediately after the King's death) makes this remark:

> "The most surprising thing about this behaviour is that the Queen should have encouraged it."

There is plenty of room for wonder, considering that Admiral Seymour had earlier wanted to marry,

Elizabeth. But Catherine was a clever woman, who had already had three husbands—Seymour was her fourth—and children. If any one would see through a boy's disguise as a girl she was the one. It is hard to imagine that Seymour's wife had not good cause for some form revenge on him of whom Hallam speaks of as a "dangerous and unprincipled man" and of whom Latimer said "he was a man farthest from the fear of God that ever I knew or heard of in England" as it was believed at the time of her death that he had poisoned his wife, the Queen dowager, to make way for a marriage with Elizabeth, with whom according to common belief he was still in love, it would be only natural that a woman of her disposition and with her sense of humour, should revenge herself in a truly wifely way by using for the purpose, without betraying the secret, her private knowledge or belief of the quasi-princess's real sex. Such would afford an infinite gratification to an ill-used wife jealous of so vain a husband.

We now come to the crux of the whole story—the touchstone of this strange eventful history. Could there have been such a boy as is told of; one answering to the many conditions above shown to be vitally necessary for the carrying out of such a scheme of imposture. The answer to this question is distinctly in the affirmative; there *could* have been such a boy; had the Duke of Richmond been born fourteen or fifteen years earlier than he was, the difficulties of appearance, intellect, education, and other qualifications need not have presented themselves.

If the question to be asked is: "Was there such a boy?" the answer cannot be so readily given. In the meantime there are some considerations from the study of which—or through which—an answer may, later, be derived.

H. THE SOLUTION

The Duke of Richmond

The points which must be settled before we can solve the mystery of the *Bisley Boy* are:

(1) Was there such an episode regarding the early life of the Princess Elizabeth?

(2) Was there such a boy as was spoken of?

(3) How could such an imposture have been carried out, implying as it did—

(a) A likeness to the Princess so extraordinary as not to have created suspicion in the mind of anyone not already in the plot.

(b) An acquaintance with the circumstances of the life of the Princess sufficiently accurate to ward off incipient suspicion caused by any overlooking or neglect of necessary conditions.

(c) An amount of education and knowledge equal to that held by a child of ten to twelve years of age who had been taught by some of the most learned persons of the time.

THE DUKE OF RICHMOND

(d) A skill in classics and foreign tongues only known amongst high scholars and diplomatists.

(e) An ease of body and a courtliness of manner and bearing utterly foreign to any not bred in the higher circles of social life.

If there could be found a boy answering such conditions—one whose assistance could be had with facility and safety—then the solution is possible, even if not susceptible of the fullest proof. Following the lines of argument hitherto used in this book, let us first consider reasons why such an argument is tenable. I may then perhaps be allowed to launch the theory which has come to me during this investigation.

(*a*) *His Birth and Appearance*

A part—and no small part—of the bitterness of Henry VIII in not having a son to succeed him was that, though he had a son, such could not by the existing law succeed him on the throne.

Nearly ten years after his marriage to Catherine of Aragon and after a son and other children had been born to them, all of whom had died shortly after birth, Henry had in the manner of mediæval kings—and others—entered on a love affair, the object of his illicit affection being one of the ladies-in-waiting to Queen Catherine, Elizabeth, daughter of John Blount of Knevet, Shropshire.

The story of this love affair is thus given in

quaint old English in *Grafton's Chronicle* first published in 1569 which covers the period from 1189 to 1558:

> "You shall understande, the King in his freshe youth was in the cheynes of love with a faire damosell called Elizabeth Blunt, daughter of Syr John Blunt Knight, which damosell in synging, daunsing, and in all goodly pastimes, excelled all other, by the which goodly pastimes, she wanne the king's hart: and she againe shewed him such favour that by him she bare a goodly man childe, of beautie like to the father and mother. This child was well brought up lyke a Princes childe."

(*b*) *His Upbringing and Marriage*

This son of an unlawful union—born in 1519 it is said—was called Henry Fitzroy after the custom applicable in such cases to the natural children of kings. Naturally enough his royal father took the greatest interest in this child and did, whilst the latter lived, all in his power to further his interests. A mere list of the honours conferred on him during his short life will afford some clue to the King's intention of his further advancement, should occasion serve. The shower of favours began in 1525 when the child, as is said, was only six years of age. On the 18th of June of this year he was created Earl of Nottingham and Duke of Richmond and Somerset, with precedence over all dukes except those of the King's lawful issue. He was also made a Knight of the Garter—of which exalted Order he was raised to the Lieutenancy eight years later. He was also nominated to other high offices: the King's Lieutenant General for districts north of the Trent; and Keeper of the city and fortress of Carlisle. To these posts were added those of Lord High Admiral of England, Wales, Ireland, Normandy, Gascony and Aquitaine; Warden General of the Marches of Scotland, and Receiver of Middleham and of Sheriff Hutton, Yorkshire. He was also given an income of four thousand pounds sterling per annum. In 1529, being then only ten years of age, he was also made Lord Lieutenant of Ireland, Constable of Dover Castle and Warden of the Cinque Ports—three of the most important offices of the Nation. A few months before his death in 1536 there was a general understanding that Henry VIII intended to make him King of Ireland and possibly to nominate him as his successor on the throne of England. That some such intention was in Henry's mind was shown by the Succession Act passed just before the close of the Parliament which was dissolved in 1536. In this Act it is fixed that the Crown is to devolve on the King's death to the son of Jane Seymour and in default of issue by him, on Mary and Elizabeth in succession in case of lack of issue by the former. In the event of their both dying before the King and without issue he is to appoint by will his successor on the throne.

The various important posts conferred on the young Duke of Richmond were evidently preparations for the highest post of all, which in default of legitimate issue of his own legitimate children he intended to confer on him.

The education which was given to the little Duke is of especial interest and ought in the present connection to be carefully studied. It was under the care of Richard Croke, celebrated for his scholarship; who in the modern branch was assisted by John Palsgrave the author of the earliest English grammar of the French language *"Lesclarcissement de la langue Francoyse."* In spite of the opposition of his household the Duke of Richmond devoted his young life to study rather than to arms. Whilst still a young boy he had already read a part of *Cæsar, Virgil* and *Terence,* knew a little Greek, and was fairly skilful in music—singing and playing on the virginals. There was much talk in Court circles as to whom he should marry and many ladies of high degree were named. One was a niece of Pope Clement VII; another was a Danish princess; still another a princess of France; also a daughter of Eleanor, dowager Queen of Portugal, a sister of Charles V. This lady was afterwards Queen of France.

Early in 1532 the Duke resided for a while at Hatfield. Then he went to Paris with his friend the Earl of Surrey, son of the Duke of Norfolk. There he remained till September, 1533. On his return to England he married by special dispensation, on 25 November, 1533, Mary Howard, daughter of the Duke of Norfolk by his second marriage and sister of Surrey. Incidentally he is said to have been present at the beheading of Queen Anne (Boleyn), May 19, 1536. He did not long survive the last-named exhibition, for some two months later—22 July, 1536, he died. There was at the time a suspicion that he had been poisoned by Lord Rochford, brother of Queen Anne (Boleyn).

Henry Duke of Richmond and Somerset had no legal issue. As a matter of fact though he was married in 1533, nearly three years before his death, he never lived with his wife. It was said that he was not only young for matrimony, being only seventeen; but was in very bad health. It was intended that after his marriage he should go to Ireland; but on account of the state of his health that journey was postponed—as it turned out, for ever.

A light on this ill-starred marriage is thrown in the quaint words of another chronicler of the time, Charles Wriothesley, who wrote of the time between 1485 and 1559.

> "But the said younge duke had never layne by his wife, and so she is maide, wife, and now a widowe; I praie God send her now good fortune."

In this summarised history certain points are to be noticed:

(1) The Duke of Richmond was like his father (Henry VIII) and his mother who was "fayre."

(2) A Dispensation was obtained for his mar-

riage to Lady Mary Howard which took place in 1533 but with whom he never cohabited.

There is a side-light here of the hereditary aspect of the case. Both the Duke and Duchess of Richmond were "fayre," and in the language of the old chroniclers "fayre" means blonde. Wintown for instance speaking of Macbeth's supposed descent from the Devil says:

"Gottyne he was on ferly wys
"Hys Modyr to woddis mad oft repayre
"For the delyte of halesum ayre.
"Swa, scho past a-pon a day
"Tyl a Wod, hyr for to play:
"Scho met at cas with a fayr man."

And Grafton thus speaks under date 7 September 1533 of Elizabeth's birth: "The Queen was delivered of a fayre Lady."

Now Anne Boleyn is described as small and lively, a brunette with black hair and beautiful eyes, and yet her daughter is given as red-haired by all the painters.

It is somewhat difficult to make out the true colours of persons. For instance Giovanni Michiel writing to the Venetian Senate in 1557 puts in his description of Elizabeth "She is tall and well formed, with a good skin, although swarthy" but in the same page he says "she prides herself on her father and glories in him; everybody is saying that she also resembles him more than the Queen [Mary] does." As to the introduction of the word "swarthy" as above; it may have been one of the tricks of Elizabeth to keep the Venetian ambassador from knowing too much or getting any ground for guessing. If so it looks rather like Elizabeth concealing her real identity—which would be an argument in favour of an imposture; if she was the real princess there would be no need for concealment.

It is only common sense to expect, if the paternal element was so strong in Henry as to reproduce in offspring his own colour, that had the Duke of Richmond had any issue especially by a fair wife it too would have inherited something of the family colour. Holbein's picture of the "Lady of Richmond," as the Duke's wife was called, shows her as a fair woman.

These are two points to be here borne in mind; that Henry VIII was probably bald, for in none of his pictures is any hair visible. It would hardly be polite to infer that Elizabeth wore a wig for the same reason. But it is recorded that she always travelled with a stock of them—no less than eighty of various colours.

But there are other indications of such concealment. Why for instance did she object to see doctors? So long as she was free and could control them she did not mind; but whilst she was under duress they were a source of danger. Perhaps it is this which accounts for her taking the Sacrament on 26 August, 1554 when she was practically a prisoner at Woodstock in the keeping of Sir Henry Bedingfield. About the third week in June the Princess asked Sir Henry to be allowed to have a doctor sent to her. He in turn applied to the Council who made answer on the 25th that the Queen's Oxford physician was ill and Mr. Wendy was absent and the remaining one, Mr. Owen, could not be spared. The latter however recommended two Oxford doctors, Barnes and Walbec, in case she should care to see either of them. On July 4th Sir Henry reported to the Council that Elizabeth in politely declining said: "I am not minded to make any stranger privy to the state of my body, but commit it to God." Then, when through her submission to the Queen's religious convictions she had obtained her liberty, she took no more concern in the matter.

The Duchess of Richmond

Thomas Howard, Duke of Norfolk, married twice. His second wife was the lady Elizabeth Stafford, eldest daughter of the Duke of Buckingham, and he had issue by both marriages. In 1533 the only surviving daughter of the second marriage was Mary, who was thus the Lady Mary Howard, sister of the Earl of Surrey. It was this lady with whom the uncompleted marriage of the Duke of Richmond took place. Doubtless they were early friends. In her youth she used to spend the summer at Tendring Hall, Suffolk, and the winter

THE DUCHESS OF RICHMOND

at Hunsdon, Hertfordshire, where was one of Henry's palaces; in addition Henry was one of the closest companions of her brother, the Earl of Surrey. Lady Richmond's part in the historical episode before us is hardly direct. It only comes in through two circumstances not unattended with mystery. It is not necessary that the two were correlated; but no student can get away from the idea that there was some connection between them, especially when there is another inference bearing on the subject with reference to the second marriage of the Duchess. This took place after an interval of some years to Gilbert, son of Sir George Talboys of Goloths, Lincolnshire. The name of the second husband is variously spelled in the chronicles as Tailboise or Talebuse. She died in the year before Elizabeth came to the throne. The two things to examine closely with regard to this marriage to the Duke of Richmond were the Dispensation for the marriage (together with the date of it), and its non-fulfilment. The Dispensation was dated 28 November, 1533, but the marriage took place three days earlier. Whether this discrepancy had anything to do with her later marriage to Talboys we can only guess—unless of course more exhaustive search can produce some document, unknown as yet, which may throw light on the subject. It is a matter of no light mystery why a Dispensation was obtained at such a time and by whom it was effected. At this time Henry

VIII was engaged in the bitterest struggle of his life, that regarding the supremacy of the Pope, so that it was a direct violation of his policy to have asked for, or even to recognise such a Dispensation in the case of his own son whom he intended to succeed him as King. Before a year had passed he had actually thrown over the Papal authority altogether, and had taken into his own hands the headship of the National Church. What then was behind such a maladroit action? If it had been done as a piece of statecraft—the ostensible showing that there was as yet no direct rupture between the British Nation and the Papacy—it would have lost its efficacy if it might be cited as a Court favour rather than a national right. Moreover, as it was to sanction by then existing canonical law a marriage of Henry's son with a daughter of the head of the most powerful Catholic House in England, it could not be expected that Rome would not use this in its strife for the continuation of its supremacy. If Henry was directly concerned in the matter, it was bad policy and unlike him to conciliate Catholicism by a yielding on the part of one who would be in the future the Head of the Reformed Church. Altogether it leaves one under the impression that there must have been a more personal cause than any yet spoken of. Something to be covered up, or from which suspicion should be averted. There was already quite enough material for a controversy in case Henry Fitzroy should come to the throne and it might be well to minimise any further risk. But in such case what was there to be covered up or from which suspicion should be averted? Already Richmond held under his father all the threads of government in his own hand. If he ever should need to tighten them it would be done by himself as ruler. There must still be some reason which must be kept secret and of which Henry himself did not and must not know. Beyond this again was the question of the personal ambition of "Bluff King Hal." It was not sufficient for him that a barren heir should succeed him—even if that heir was his own son. He wanted to found a dynasty, and if he suspected for an instant that after all his plotting and striving—all his titanic efforts to overcome such obstacles as nations and religions—his hopes might fail through lack of issue on his son's part he would cease to waste his time and efforts on his behalf. It is almost impossible to imagine that the Duke of Richmond had not had *some* love affairs—if indeed he was only seventeen (of which there is a doubt)—it must be borne in mind that both the Lancastrians and the Yorkists who united in the Tudor stock matured early. On both his father's and mother's side Henry Fitzroy was of a pleasure-loving, voluptuous nature, and as the masculine element predominated in his make-up there is not any great stretch of imagination required to be satisfied that there was some young likeness of him toddling or running about. But in a case like his masculine mis-doing does not count; it is only where a woman's credit is at stake that secrecy is a vital necessity. We must therefore look to the female side to find a cause for any mystery which there may be. So far as a boy of the right age is concerned with a decided likeness to Henry VIII it would not have required much searching about to lay hands on a suitable one.

But here a new trouble would begin. It would be beyond nature to expect that any mother would consent, especially at a moment's notice, to her child running such a risk as the substitute of the dead Princess Elizabeth was taking, without some kind of assurance or guarantee of his safety. Moreover, if there were other relatives, they would be sure to know, and some of them to make trouble unless their mouths were closed. Practically the only chance of carrying such an enterprise through would be if the substitute were an orphan or in a worse position—one whose very life was an embarrassment to those to whom it should be most dear.

Here opens a field for romantic speculation. Such need not clash with history which is a record of fact. Call it romance if we will; indeed until we have more perfect records we must. If invention is to be called in to the aid of deduction no one can complain if these two methods of exercise of intellect are kept apart and the boundaries between them are duly charted. Any speculation beyond this can be only regarded as belonging to the region of pure fiction.

In one way there is a duty which the reader must not shirk, if only on his own account: not to refuse to accept facts without due consideration. Wildly improbable as the Bisley story is, it is not impossible. Whoever says, offhand, that such a story is untrue on the face of it ought to study the account of a death reported at Colchester in Essex just a hundred years ago. A servant died who had been in the same situation as housemaid and nurse for thirty years. But only after death was the true sex of the apparent woman discovered. It was masculine!

Here I must remind such readers as honour my work with their attention that I am venturing merely to tell a tradition sanctioned by long time, and that I only give as comments historical facts which may be tested by any student. I have invented and shall invent nothing; and only claim the same right which I have in common with every one else—that of forming my own opinion.

Here it is that we may consider certain additions to the original Bisley tradition. How these are connected with the main story is impossible to say after the lapse of centuries; but in all probability there is a basis of ancient belief in all that has been added. The following items cover the additional ground.

When the governess wished to hide the secret hurriedly, she hid the body, intending it to be only temporarily, in the stone coffin which lay in the garden at Overcourt outside the Princess's window.

Some tens of years ago the bones of a young girl lying amidst rags of fine clothing were found in the stone coffin.

The finder was a churchman—a man of the highest character and a member of a celebrated ecclesiastical family.

The said finder firmly believed in the story of the Bisley Boy.

Before Elizabeth came to the throne all those who knew the secret of the substitution were in some way got rid of or their silence assured.

The name of the substituted youth was Neville; or such was the name of the family with whom he was living at the time.

There are several persons in the neighbourhood of Bisley who accept the general truth of the story even if some of the minor details appear at first glance to be inharmonious. These persons are not of the ordinary class of gossipers, but men and women of light and leading who have fixed places in the great world and in the social life of their own neighbourhood. With some of them the truth of the story is an old belief which makes a tie with any new investigator.

The Unfulfilled Marriage

The remaining point to touch on is the unfulfilled marriage of the Duke of Richmond. This certainly needs some explanation, or else the mystery remains dark as ever.

Here we have two young persons of more than fair presence, and graced with all the endearing qualities that the mind as well as the eye can grasp. We have the assurance of Chronicles regarding Henry Fitzroy; and from Holbein's picture we can judge for ourselves of the lady's merits. They are both well-to-do. The lady, one of title, daughter of one of the most prominent Dukes in England, the man then holding many of the most important posts in the State, and with every expectation of wearing in due course the purple of royalty. They both come of families of which other members have been notorious for amatory episodes; voluptuousness is in their blood. They have been old friends—and yet when they marry they at once separate, she going to her own folk and he to Windsor. Seemingly they do not meet again in the two and a half years that elapse before his death. The story about his youth and health preventing cohabitation is all moonshine. The affair points to the likelihood of some ante-matrimonial liaison of which, as yet, we know nothing. Applying the experiences of ordinary life in such cases, we can easily believe that Mary Howard, egged on by her unscrupulous and ambitiously-intriguing brother, was for ulterior purposes either forced or helped into an intrigue with the young Duke. There is no doubt that Surrey was unscrupulous enough for it. A similar design on his part—only infinitely more base—cost him his head. He had tried to induce his sister, Duchess of Richmond, to become mistress of Henry VIII—her own father-in-law!—so that she might have power over him; and it does not seem that there was any wonderful indignation on the part of the lady at the shameful proposal.

We are told that when Sir John Gates and Sir Richard Southwell, the royal Commissioners for examining witnesses in the case of the charge of treason against the Duke of Norfolk and the Earl of Surrey, arrived at Kenninghall in the early morning and made known their general purposes in coming, the Duchess of Richmond "almost fainted." But all the same when she knew more exactly what they wanted she promised without any forcing to tell all she knew. As a matter of fact her evidence (with that of Elizabeth Holland, the mistress of the Duke of Norfolk), whilst it helped to get Norfolk off, aided in condemning Surrey. There must have been some other cause for her consternation. She had been bred up in the midst of intrigues, polemical and dynastic as well as of personal ambition, and was well inured to keeping her countenance as well as her head in moments of stress. The cause of her "almost fainting" must have been something which concerned her even more nearly than either father or brother. It could only have been fear for her child or herself—or for both. It is possible that she dreaded discovery of some sort. *Omne ignotum pro magnifico.* Suspicion has long flexible tentacula, with eyes and ears at the end of them, which can penetrate everywhere and see and hear everything. She knew how to dread suspicion and to fear the consequences which must result from inquiry or investigation of any sort. If she had had a child it must have been kept hidden, and if possible far away—as the unknown Boy was at Bisley. Indeed the Howards had immense family ramifications and several of them had collateral relationships in and about Bisley. There were Nevilles there, and doubtless some of them were poor relations relegated to the far away place where living was cheap and where they might augment their tenuous incomes by taking in even poorer relations than themselves whose rich relatives wished to hide them away. It is only a surmise; but if there had been a case of a child unaccounted for, which any member of so great a family as the Howards wished to keep dark, it would be hard to find a more favourable locality than the little almost inaccessible hamlet in the Cotswolds. If there were such a child, how easy it would all have been. When the Duke was married he was fourteen or perhaps sixteen at most—an age which though over-young for fatherhood in the case of ordinary men seemed to offer to the Plantagenet-York-Lancaster blood no absolute difficulty of taking up such responsibility. As Elizabeth was only born some two months before the Duke's marriage there was not any time to spare—a fact which would doubtless have been used to his advantage if Henry's natural son had lived. In all probability Richmond's marriage was a part of the plot for aggrandisement of the Howards which began with the unscrupulous securing by Surrey of the son of Henry VIII at the cost of his sister's honour; and ended with the death of Surrey as a traitor—a doom which his father only escaped by the King dying whilst the Act of Attainder was lying ready for his signature. If this reasoning be correct—though the data on which it is founded be meagre and without actual proof—as yet—the risk of Duchess Mary's child born before her marriage must have been a terrible hazard. On one side perhaps the most powerful sceptre in the world as guerdon; on the other death and ruin of the child on which such hopes were built. No wonder then that Duchess Mary "almost fainted" when in the early dawn the King's Commissioners conveyed to her the broad object of their coming. No wonder that freed by larger knowledge from the worst apprehension which could be for her, she announced her willingness to conceal nothing that she knew. That promise could not and would not have been made had the whole range of possibilities, which as yet no one suspected, been opened to their investigation. For even beyond the concern which she felt from the arbitrary power of the King and at the remorseless grip of the law, she had reason to doubt her own kin—the nearest of them—in such a struggle as was going on around them when the whole of the Empire, the Kingdom of England, France and Spain, and the Papacy were close to the melting-pot. It would have been but a poor look-out for a youth of a little more than a dozen years of age had fate made him the shuttlecock of such strenuous players who did not hold "fair play" as a primary rule of the game in which they were engaged.

In his *Life of Elizabeth,* Gregario Leti concludes a panegyric on the Queen's beauty with the following: "This was accompanied by such inward qualities that those who knew her were accustomed to say that heaven had given her such rare qualities that she was doubtless reserved for some great work in the world." The Italian historian perhaps "builded better than he knew," for whether the phrase applies to the one who is supposed to have occupied the throne or one who did so occupy it, it is equally true. The world at that crisis wanted just such an one as Elizabeth. All honour to her whosoever she may have been, boy or girl matters not.

INDEX